Managing IT Innovation for Business Value

IT Best Practices Series

IT Best Practices Series

This book is published as a part of the IT Best Practices Series at Intel Press. Books in this series focus on managing information technology investments to produce measured business value. Business value indicators include financial metrics such as return on investment, operational metrics such as inventory turns, and productivity metrics such as reduced time to complete tasks.

Information technology investments include network and server infrastructure, business systems, engineering systems, and personal productivity systems. Business value can be obtained when mature technologies are deployed thoughtfully and also when new technologies emerge that provide new capabilities.

This series primarily reflects the experiences of Intel's IT organization, which are complemented with experiences of other IT organizations. Examples and case studies are included to show how business value manifests itself in different companies and industries.

For detailed information about these and other books, as well as announcements of forthcoming books in the series, visit the Intel Press Web site: *www.intel.com/intelpress*.

IMPORTANT

You can access the companion Web site for this book on the Internet at:

www.intel.com/intelpress/inov

Use the serial number located in the upper-right hand corner of the last page in the book to register your book and access additional material, including the Digital Edition version.

Managing IT Innovation for Business Value

Practical Strategies for IT and Business Managers

Esther Baldwin
Martin Curley

Intel PRESS

ISBN 1-934053-04-X

Publisher: Richard Bowles

Managing Editor: David King
Program Manager: Stuart Douglas
Text Design and Composition: Phoebus Group, LLP
Graphic Art: Richard Eberly (illustrations), Richard Eberly and Ted Cyrek (cover)

Library of Congress Cataloging in Publication Data:

Printed in China

10 9 8 7 6 5 4 3 2 1

To my mother, Violet,
who often embodied innovation,
my brothers and sisters,
my daughter and grandchildren,
and loved ones.

— Esther Baldwin

To my wife, Ann,
and my children, Ciana, Clodagh, Aoibhe, and Liam,
and my parents, Brendan and Peig.

— Martin Curley

Contents

9   Launching Systemic IT Innovation   149

Appendix A Case Studies in IT Innovation 163

Foreword

The management of innovation has been a distinguishing feature for Intel Corporation since its founding. While we at Intel have focused much of our innovation efforts on component, microprocessor and systems architecture innovation, we have recognized the importance of helping catalyze and enable technology-led business innovation as well. Indeed as technology advances, one could argue that a new discipline is emerging called IT Innovation or, alternatively, Services Innovation, which uses the power of information technology to deliver new services. Services are at the core of the economic growth of most advanced economies, and information technology is at the core of much services innovation.

I am pleased to see that Esther Baldwin and Martin Curley have captured and cultivated the Intel IT organization's innovation experience in this book. It is a stated objective for our IT professionals to share their experiences as broadly as possible. The many examples in this book, both from Intel and from others, stand as proof points underscoring the importance of being innovative.

Intel employees are methodical and Martin and Esther are no exception. Innovation is not simply the random act of having a bright idea. Rather, innovation can and should be a systematic process supported by methods and tools. The authors provide strong models for rationalizing the innovation process. They also include techniques for accelerating adoption, which is a critically important step.

This book addresses two complementary roles for IT and innovation:

■ With techniques such as user experience design and tools such as rapid solution prototyping, the authors show how innovative IT services and capabilities can be developed and deployed. Innovation thus leads to new services and better IT.

■ Esther and Martin also show how the IT organization can foster innovation across the enterprise by providing innovation infrastructure, workshops, and assessment instruments. Thus, IT leads to better innovation.

Information technology is a powerful set of tools and techniques capable of transforming the way we live and work. Using IT to accelerate innovation and adoption is a profoundly important insight.

— Justin Rattner, Chief Technical Officer, Intel Corporation

Acknowledgments

Writing a book about innovation and IT after years of work at Intel Corporation inevitably means that we have a good number of people to acknowledge. When he was praised for inventing the calculus, Isaac Newton said, "I stood on the shoulders of giants." And so it is true for us. The vibrant and challenging culture at Intel has provided us with a rich and varied set of experiences.

We begin at home and thank our families for the patience they have offered as we researched, wrote, and rewrote this book and their influence in our lives. For Martin, it is Ann and their children—Ciana, Clodagh, Aoibhe, and Liam—for the constant joy that they bring and their patience with his late nights and trips away from home, and also his parents, Brendan and Peig, and his brothers and sisters. For Esther, it is her parents, Harry and Vi Baldwin, her daughter Esther Kristina Anderson, and grandchildren, Antonia and Alexandra. We appreciate the patience of our loved ones from whom we have been sometimes absent while we wrote this book.

PhoebusGroup, comprising Susan and David King, worked as our editors and, in addition to bringing industry expertise, focus, and energy, they also brought friendship and comfort to the writing process with gourmet meals, and Northwest cultural experiences. Our authors' retreats to Astoria, Oregon, were both productive and enjoyable. David's and Susan's constancy of purpose and complete focus made sure that the book met its schedule, and they made a huge contribution to its delivery.

We would also like to acknowledge Richard Eberly, our illustrator, for rendering our ideas so artfully.

Leadership

We would like to acknowledge and thank the people who have provided leadership through vision, action, and skin-in-the-game of innovation: Gene Meieran, our *Innovation Fellow*, innovation thought leader, pathfinder, and unstinting supporter; Doug Busch for his vision, risk taking, and leadership when supporting the IT Innovation and Research team, driving IT as a value centre, and providing ongoing direction and innovations, such as the concept car program, innovation sabbaticals, and role-modeling management commitment; Herman D'Hooge for leading user-centered innovation and design at Intel, partnering with us, and supporting us; Justin Rattner for his leadership, sponsorship, collaboration, and powerful influence that opened doors for us in the academic community and from whom we learned Intel's Research process; Chris Thomas for his strategy insights and expertise at finding paths to solve the challenges of the next billion PC innovators; Will Swope for supporting the use of Intel IT Innovation centres as Intel Innovation centres; John Davies, for realizing that IT innovation can contribute to the bottom line at Intel and for providing us with the opportunities to do so.

Thanks to Christian Morales and Gordon Graylish in EMEA for their confidence in using the EMEA IT Innovation centres to enable demand-side innovation in the region. And, thanks to all the site leaders around the world for their vision of, and tangible support for, the Innovation Centres.

Innovation Tools and Practices

The authors would like to acknowledge the many talented innovation practitioners and friends who have contributed their expertise, provided new integral processes and solutions, and stimulated our thinking to explore untapped avenues. They include Joe Hegarty and Shuki Parchef for management commitment expertise, negotiation leadership, and Innovation Centre start-up tools and methodology such as asset management.

Thanks to Jim Kelly for his game-changing SIfT workshop that is helping prove the business value of innovation as a process; Kenny He and Scott Huskey for their user-centered design research and practices; Jo Moore and Jo Rowe for their competency training and development expertise; Linda April, Deanna Nunley, Dan Liu, and Alice Brennan for their marketing and communications partnership, systems, and expertise. We thank Ron Miller and Janet Gluck for the IT@Intel tools and support they have provided over the years, Eleanor Wynn, David Hartley,

Phil Tierney, and Don Littlefield for their contribution to the first innovation portal vision and mock up; Amir Rogel for being our TRIZ master; Abram Detofsky and Annie Frost for providing socialization structure and tools for us as innovation practitioners; and Dan Liu for helping us maintain a global perspective.

We thank Malvina Nisman for her dedicated and disciplined approach to innovation operations and pipeline management; Esther Anderson for her insights into trend predictors; our technical supporters Tony Corrigan, Eddie Wong, and James O'Neill, who turned our virtual environment vision into reality; Peg Ryan and the Intel Developer's Forum team for their vision to include IT Innovation as an ongoing topic; and, finally, Brendan Cannon, Dan Etheredge, and Polly Herren for sharing their cases.

This list would not be complete without Pat Gelsinger, John Johnson, Don MacDonald, Sean Maloney, Steve Pawlowksi, Justin Rattner, Bill Siu, Gregg Wyant—colleagues whom we interviewed to draw from their experience.

Martin wishes to acknowledge co-author Esther's enthusiasm and focus in ensuring that this book actually got written. Esther's Liverpool humor and her continuous stream of ideas combined with knowledge from her extensive network helped make this a better book.

Esther wishes to acknowledge Martin's sense of humor, which makes him a pleasure to work with, his knowledge of industry leaders and experts, and his energy in working several jobs: Directing Global IT Innovation and Research at Intel, co-founding and directing the Innovation Value Institute at the National University of Ireland, and co-authoring this book, all while working on his doctoral dissertation and being a family man.

Lastly, we would like to thank Rich Bowles and Stuart Douglas for their unstinting support and contributions; without them, this book would not be in your hands.

Esther Baldwin
Martin Curley
October 2007

Chapter 1

Introduction

Innovation is the specific instrument of entrepreneurship. It is the act that endows resources with a new capacity to create wealth.
—Peter F. Drucker

Innovation is the creation and adoption of something new that creates value for the organization that adopts it. When narrowly defined, the primary goal of innovation is new product development. When defined more broadly, as it is in this book, opportunities to innovate and create business value permeate the organization. Opportunities to build innovative information technology (IT) solutions methodically and to deploy these solutions quickly are especially attractive, and that is one focus of this book. The second focus is on IT systems that support innovation across the enterprise. We describe our *innovation enabling service environment,* which is in the process of diffusing across Intel.

For some, innovation necessarily implies that an entirely new idea is required, as if innovation were entirely equivalent to invention. We believe that innovation also includes the reapplication of existing ideas in different contexts. Across the organization at Intel, we seek out best known methods (BKMs). For example, to guide Intel Corporation's investments, we developed a strategic long-range planning process as a BKM. Reapplying this same planning process to guide the investments of the IT organization can be considered an innovation.

New ideas with the potential to create value can fail to do so, usually because of problems with adoption. New ideas, clever products, and helpful IT solutions that do not find their way into usage, for whatever reason, cannot deliver business value. Innovation theorists such as Everett Rogers (2003) believe that adoption is driven by *diffusion*, which they believe to be primarily a social process. We have more to say about diffusion later in the book.

Table 1.1   Impact of Maturity in Innovation Capability

Maturity Level	Who sees the innovations?	Who benefits from the innovations?	How do they benefit?
Optimizing	Industry	Shareholders	Increased shareholder value, stock appreciation, higher dividends, willingness to invest
Advanced	Executives	Customers	Needs are met, customers are satisfied, loyal, and committed
Intermediate	Managers	Company	Growth, new markets open, image and reputation enhanced, increased revenues and markets, higher retention of employees and customers, greater longevity
Basic	All employees	All employees	New job opportunities, greater job satisfaction, recognition and rewards, creative workspace, higher energy, and a sense of ownership
Initial	Individuals and managers responsible for R&D and incubators	R&D's individuals and managers	Big wins, which occur occasionally in unstructured environments, receive recognition and rewards

Source: Intel IT

The Importance of Innovation

Innovation is a capability that can help companies stay ahead of their competition and exceed their customers' and stockholders' expectations. Executed poorly or not at all, IT innovation can cause a company to fall behind and trigger a decision by the CIO to replace IT professionals, perhaps with outsource providers with demonstrated expertise. IT innovation helps IT personnel keep their jobs.

IT innovation is especially important because it is a pervasive enabler of business processes. Thus, innovative IT capabilities fuel the agility and efficiency of the entire company. In addition to traditional IT systems such as enterprise resource planning (ERP), innovative IT systems now reach out to customers to provide services.

Innovation is increasingly visible as it matures, and the importance of innovation increases in proportion to how different audiences value it. Like quality and safety, innovation is becoming a new standard with which employees, company executives, customers, and shareholders evaluate the company.

As Table 1.1 shows, the audience expands in scope as innovation capability matures, that is, as companies progress from basic innovation capabilities to optimizing ones. The same is true when innovation capability becomes a competitive advantage. Table 1.1 also identifies who sees and benefits from innovation and how benefits take form. Benefits can be tangible, such as a monetary reward, or intangible when emotional or perceived.

Innovation's Virtuous Circle

Innovation is a key ingredient to longevity and survival, according to Arie de Geus (1997). Innovation is indeed about delivering value and, more importantly, innovation capabilities enable companies to build the future and adapt to change. New ideas need to be cultivated constantly, to mitigate or counter economic, political, competitive, and industry risks.

When innovation capabilities mature, they foster a virtuous circle, as shown in Figure 1.2. Satisfied customers remain loyal, stockholders are rewarded, the company is successful, and employees are energetic and capable innovators.

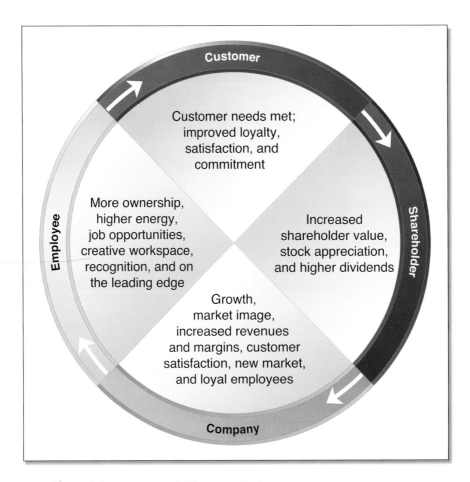

Figure 1.1 Innovation's Virtuous Circle

Source: Intel Corporation

Three Types of Innovation

To sharpen your thinking about innovation, consider the following categories: radical innovation, incremental innovation, and innovation by reapplication.

Radical Innovation

Radical innovations fundamentally change an industry and our daily lives. These innovations define entirely new categories of devices and processes. Radical innovations are often closely associated with the innovator. Examples include Edison's light bulb, Alberto Santos-Dumont's airplane, and Lin Yutang's typewriter. In IT, radical innovations include Charles Babbage's concept of a programmable computer, Alan Turing's Turing machine, Grace Hopper's Flow-Matic compiler, and Robert Metcalfe's co-invention of the Ethernet protocol.

Incremental Innovation

Incremental innovations improve on radical innovations. These innovations are often associated with companies. Bell's phone leads to AT&T, Edison's light bulb morphs to General Electric, and Boeing improves greatly on Santos-Dumont's plane. In IT, the mouse is a ubiquitous pointing device, and Cisco and many others provide Ethernet hubs and routers. Moore's law describes incremental innovation of microprocessor performance. Incremental innovation creates enormous benefits for successful companies, whereas radical innovators rarely benefit greatly beyond their initial invention.

Innovation by Reapplication

Other innovations are existing concepts or solutions operating in one domain that are applied to new domains. A non-IT example is the modification of *Super Glue* chemistry to make a liquid stitch for medicine. In IT, software designed for three-dimensional architectural design can be reapplied to other three-dimensional design needs, such as mechanical design. A knowledge management system constructed to manage product documentation can also be used to track market data. A version-control system designed for software development can be repurposed for engineering and documentation version control. Especially in IT, the opportunity to reapply applications is common, and because reapplied innovations reuse existing applications, they are far less expensive to deliver.

Innovation Need Not be Wholescale Invention

While radical innovations are inventions, incremental innovations and innovations that reapply known solutions to new problems are not. Especially in business, incremental innovations are highly valued because they add value on top of a sunk cost. Companies that can create new and improved products stand on the shoulders of prior investment.

Table 1.2 The Ten Types of Innovation

Innovation Category	Innovation Type	Description of Type	Intel Examples
Finance	Business Model	How you make money	Intel: Not processors, but platforms Intel IT: 100% ebusiness
	Networks and Alliances	How you join forces with other companies for mutual benefit	Intel: Founder of Sematech, member of Supplier Network Intel IT: Active with itshare.org
Process	Enabling Process	How you support the company's core processes and workers	Intel: Support global standards, e.g., WiMAX Intel IT: Global standardized IT infrastructure to support distant collaboration
	Core Processes	How you create and add value to your offerings	Intel: 300mm wafers reduce cost by 30% Intel IT: Move processor design to Intel Architecture and Open Source to save $1B
Offerings	Product Performance	How you design your core offering	Intel: Shift to multicore design for low power and high performance Intel IT: Provide idea capture and management to strategic planning team
	Product System	How you link or provide a platform for multiple products	Intel: Same cores support different processors Intel IT: Uniform handling of knowledge management
	Service	How you provide value to customers and customers beyond and around your products	Intel: Account representatives aimed at customers beyond the products Intel IT: Demonstration systems such as skoool™ content delivery technology reach beyond typical customers
Delivery	Channel	How you get your offerings to market	Intel: Multi-channel, differentiation by channel Intel IT: Early access to IT innovations at IT Innovation Zone intranet site
	Brand	How you communicate your offerings	Intel: Intel Inside® brand Intel IT: Showcase IT Innovation Centres both physical and virtual
	Customer Experience	How your customers feel when they interact with your company and its offerings	Intel: Online demonstration of multicore processing to invoke confidence in the technology Intel IT: Ethnographic study and user experience design to guide innovation

Source: Category, Type and Description, the Doblin Group; Intel Examples, Intel

We believe that reuse and thoughtful recombination of available technologies are powerful ways to innovate. At a fundamental level, IT solutions are based on storing, searching, sorting, calculating, and presenting information to users. Radical inventions such as the relational database model and the graphical user interface are highly generalizable. Assembling these ingredients to address a business problem or streamline a business process will deliver significant value.

Innovation is Not Just About Products and Services

Larry Keeley is co-founder and chief executive officer of the Doblin Group, a Chicago-based consulting company specializing in innovation. Keeley has identified ten different types of innovation, which are grouped under four broad classes of business functions, as shown in Table 1.2. Those who focus innovation narrowly on product performance, which is common in some companies, miss nine other opportunities to put new ideas to work.

Using Keeley's framework, we sorted through our Intel and Intel IT experiences to provide examples for each of the ten types. As the examples demonstrate, innovation is pervasive, and the opportunity to improve business practices with IT systems can occur for all ten types. We encourage our readers to ponder Keeley's types and generate opportunities at their own companies.

Over a six-year period, Keeley and his colleagues at Doblin have studied more than four hundred firms in more than 60 industries. Using the ten types, they surveyed investments and cumulative payback. Their findings are shown in Figure 1.2 and Figure 1.3. An interesting pattern emerged.

Investment in Innovation

According to Keeley, innovation could be applied to the finance function by developing new business models or by improving networking with trading partners, but as Figure 1.2 shows, innovation effort is not typically high for these business processes. Similarly, innovation effort is relatively low for seeking improvements to a company's enabling and core processes. Effort expended to improve delivery components such as the sales channel, brand equity, and to improve the customer's experience is also typically low.

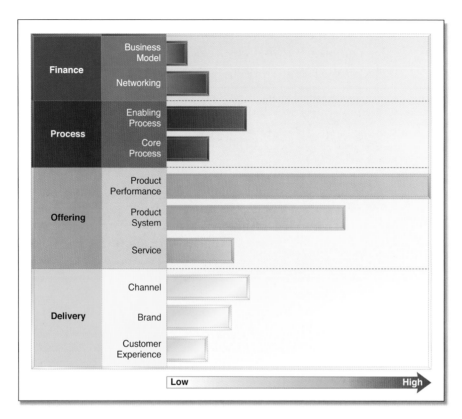

Figure 1.2 Investment in Innovation for Ten Opportunities

Source: Adapted from The Doblin Group (2006)

Innovation is most typically identified as a critical feature for product development and, more specifically, for product performance. Enterprises invest most heavily in finding new ideas about the capacity, speed, strength, or durability of their products. Performance will manifest itself in different ways for different industries. For printing engines, dots-per-inch resolution might emerge as a performance indicator, while agricultural equipment performance will likely be judged on reliability and durability.

Value Creation Opportunities

Keeley and the Doblin Group surveyed these same companies and classified cumulative payback by innovation type. The results of this research is shown in Figure 1.3. A dramatically different picture emerges.

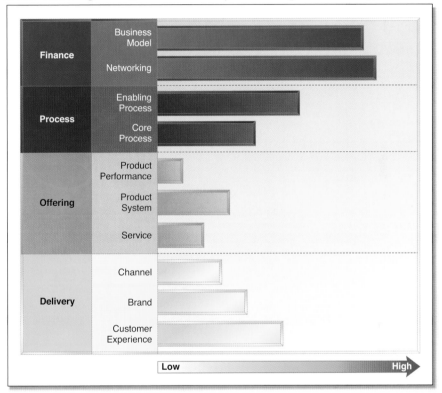

Figure 1.3 Cumulative Value Creation over Ten Years

Source: Adapted from the Doblin Group (2006)

■ One major finding is that innovative effort in the finance functions can lead to dramatic returns. A new business model, which is a new way to make money, can pay back handsomely. Improvements in the company's networking and alliances also pays back significantly.

■ The second major finding is that improvements in product performance lead to the lowest cumulative return on investment. Perhaps returns are lower for product performance because innovation is not well managed.

Findings such as these are consistent with our thinking about IT innovation. IT is pervasive in today's organizations, both large and small. Innovations targeting improvements in customer satisfaction or supporting a new business model are highly likely to pay back the IT organization and the enterprise as a whole.

Open Innovation and the Drive for Best End Value

Henry Chesbrough (2003) provides another important perspective on innovations of any kind. The traditional lifecycle model is ordinarily portrayed as a funnel with fuzzy ideas arriving from research activities at universities and industrial laboratories. Within the walls of the enterprise, the R&D group studies how these ideas might be used to create new or improved products for the company. As these ideas mature, some are set aside and others are combined into useful components, processes, methods, devices, etc. Innovation managers draw the line, narrow the funnel, and make the necessary investment decisions as research hands off demonstrated results to the development team.

Chesbrough's major contribution, shown in Figure 1.4, is illustrated by the wire-form funnel. It is Chesbrough's contention that ideas can also enter the product development lifecycle from outside the company. In fact, he would argue, successful companies are those that actively pursue intellectual property and innovative component technologies from outside the enterprise walls.

The primary determinant of successful innovation is best end value. This is often achieved by harvesting ideas from others, identifying valuable end states, and establishing exit points. Licensing innovative components from others relatively late in their lifecycle can accelerate the development process as well.

When focusing only on products as an end value, what happens to all the other good but unused ideas? Are they bad ideas? Might they have value? Instead of managing ideas in the pipeline to a single end state, Chesbrough suggests managing them to end values, some of which will be outside the enterprise. As part of the vetting process in pipeline management, all possible end values should be considered. A company can license, sell, or create a simulation for use as a sales tool, for example.

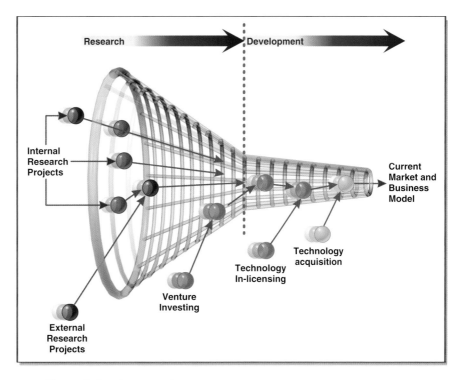

Figure 1.4 Chesbrough's Open Innovation Model

Source: Adapted from Chesbrough (2006)

While Chesbrough's model applies to all kinds of innovation, it has some interesting implications for IT innovation. Namely, licensing and assembling IT components in innovative ways is far more practical than engaging in research or foundation development. The point is obvious with respect to hardware; few companies would ever consider manufacturing special-purpose servers, for example. (Google is an interesting exception.) The implication for software is more profound. Coding solutions from scratch is rarely a good idea. To see why, read *Innovative eSupport at Intel*. The case study can be found in Appendix A on page 172.

We also believe that the open innovation model requires IT support; that is, IT is uniquely positioned to build systems that track innovations throughout the company, monitor their development, and provide the information necessary to decide which is the best end value.

Innovation Shifts in Business Models

Highly successful enterprises often thrive on shifts in an industry's underlying business model. A business model, as Keeley defines it, is how a company earns its money. In the United States, Southwest Airlines demonstrated that offering lower-cost, no-frills, direct flights to secondary metropolitan airports was a viable business model. Ticketing need not require seat assignments, thus saving time as passengers more quickly board the planes. Internet access to create boarding passes further streamlines the departure process. Less expensive, classless passenger service without meals was found to be acceptable to a wide audience of travellers.

Building incrementally on Southwest's experience, Ireland's airline, Ryanair, found other ways to change the business model. Rather than paying landing fees at smaller airports in Europe, Ryanair asks for and receives a fee. The airport and the ecosystem of stores, restaurants, and transportation services gain a steady stream of customers, thus justifying an investment that supports Ryanair. Ryanair, in turn, can lower the cost of tickets even further, making the no-frills choice difficult for customers to ignore.

In the PC market, Dell Corporation's business model collects payment before delivery and relies heavily on IT to do so. IT systems provide sophisticated infrastructure and modeling tools that allow market planners to identify buying trends, simulate changes to operations, and prepare for the short product lifecycles prevalent in the PC industry.

IT Innovation: A Two-Part Process

A successful IT innovative effort has two distinct phases. First, new solutions must be created for supporting enterprise strategies and objectives. Second, these new solutions must be adopted and diffused throughout the user community.

Creation

There is much to know about the systemic creation of new IT solutions. Successful companies develop ways to methodically identify inefficiencies and weaknesses in enterprise functioning and then to seek innovative IT solutions. Areas such as customer satisfaction provide rich opportunities to explore how IT systems might improve a company's reputation and streamline problem-solving (e.g., product support and the help desk function). Techniques such as prototyping are crucial to ensure that a potential improvement can, in fact, be fielded successfully.

Adoption and Diffusion

It is our belief that adoption and diffusion of innovative IT solutions is the more challenging half of the overall process. The root of the problem is a fundamental tension between the need to make IT efficient and to make IT better, which is illustrated in Figure 1.5.

IT Efficiency and IT Innovation

It it widely and correctly believed that new, innovative IT systems require investment, carry a measure of risk, and only become efficient over time. It is less widely appreciated that legacy systems also require investments, carry risk, and become more efficient over time when efficiency is measured year-over-year with the same technology in place. These understandings naturally lead to a tension among IT staff and IT managers assigned to address different goals. Unfortunately, some of this tension can also disrupt and confuse the investment decision making process when business and financial managers view these tensions and puzzle over them.

What is needed is a sense of balance. As Figure 1.6, shows, the balance is unlikely to be fifty-fifty. For organizations with ongoing core business systems, then the balance point will place greater resources in support of efficiency. We would argue, however, that some percentage of IT investment ought to be dedicated to accelerating the deployment of innovative IT solutions.

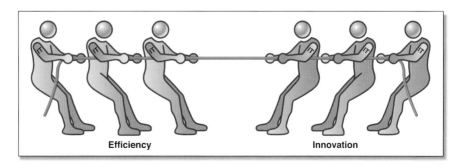

Figure 1.5 IT Efficiency vs. IT Innovation

Source: Intel Corporation

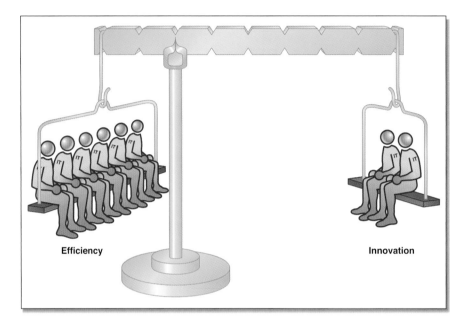

Figure 1.6 IT Efficiency Balanced with IT Innovation

Source: Intel Corporation

The balance point is affected by variables that may be different from company to company, such as the tolerance of the IT leadership for change and risk, the ratio of IT investment to corporate revenue, or the level at which competitors are using IT innovation as a strategic weapon.

IT Efficiency and IT Obsolescence

Innovation is particularly critical to IT organizations because of the high rate of change in IT capabilities. There is no practical way to maintain state-of-the-art technologies when next year's server will offer higher performance at a lower cost. The critical question is, "What are the right 'lag times' for your IT systems?" and a related question is, "What are the risks and opportunity costs associated with the lag times?"

In the late 1980s, using the Internet for electronic commerce was an innovation that reshaped some industries. A year or two of lag time left some companies with smaller market share. The risk that a competitor would leverage this new medium was significant and the opportunity cost was appreciable.

Today, technologies such as radio frequency identifier (RFID) offer potential and innovators are finding ways to put this technology to work. (See, for example, *Improved Throughput at St. Vincent's Hospital* in Sward 2006.)

Copy-Exactly

One important way to leverage innovations is to diffuse them actively with a process we call *copy-exactly*. The idea grew out of Intel's manufacturing strategy. When we issue laptop computers, for example, we standardize the hardware, operating environment, and software so that an entire group of people have identical systems. Copy-exactly accelerates the diffusion process and, at the same time, it simplifies system maintenance and user training.

Identical Fabs at Intel

When Intel develops its next-generation fab, it is engineered to specification, put into operation, and tested thoroughly. This fab becomes the standard for new fabs in other parts of the world.

After the first fab is running successfully, exact replicates of the first fab are built at other locations. Intel engineers and business managers monitor key indicators including yield, spend on materials, and excursion avoidance to measure success.

When *copy-exactly* succeeded for the fab, the technique was used to deploy assembly-and-test facilities, and then to the overall construction of the factory. When copy-exactly was reapplied to construction at Intel, for second and subsequent fab facilities, the cost per square foot was reduced by half.

The main point about copy-exactly is not simply that an innovation is copied to everyone. What is important is that production systems harvest research investments in every way. When research systems are engineered to meet the high standards needed for production, exact copies will be easier and faster to distribute. Distribution is more likely to be to be successful and maintenance more efficient.

The cost of customization goes down when we identify users with similar needs. At Intel, for example, we support engineering requirements separately from employees at large, but we still copy exactly within the engineering community.

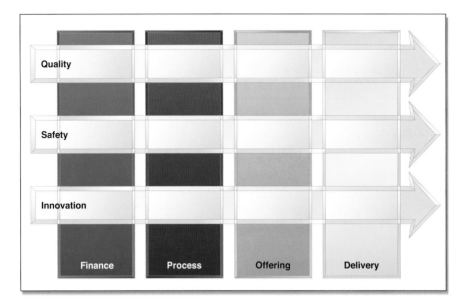

Figure 1.7 Quality, Safety, and Innovation As Lateral Processes

Source: Intel Corporation

Innovation as a Lateral Process

Innovation can be managed as a lateral process that reaches across all business functions and a portfolio of IT solutions. Without lateral management, pockets of activity are poorly supported and innovation may or may not align with enterprise objectives.

As Figure 1.7 illustrates, innovation can be managed just as quality and safety are managed in well-run organizations.

In earlier days, corporations managed quality haphazardly until they realized that an enterprise-wide approach was needed. To use Keeley's dimensions, quality was not just about the company's *offerings*, but also about *finance, process*, and *delivery*. All systems, IT and otherwise, need to reflect quality. When managing quality enterprise-wide, quality becomes an intrinsic part of the business. In a similar manner and for the same reasons, safety has emerged as a lateral process as well.

When planning our management strategies for Intel IT, we studied quality and safety management. We believe that innovation and diffusion will be far more effective when managed in a similar way. Haphazard innovation can quickly turn into tinkering, especially in an IT department filled with clever engineers. We also believe that lateral management will lead to systemic innovation, which, like quality and safety, will become an integral part of the company's culture and values.

> ### Innovation versus Tinkering
>
> Copy-exactly and lateral management are methods to avoid tinkering. At its best, tinkering is inefficient, and at its worst, it presents a risk, especially in the IT environment. Small improvements to applications applied locally and without documentation can and do raise the cost of maintenance and can even cause system outages.
>
> Communicating the importance of copy-exactly can be a management challenge. Users need to understand the boundaries within which they must remain. IT personnel need to understand the purposes and benefits of the approach. And finally, places are needed where innovation is allowed and where new ideas can be stored and evaluated.

Barriers to Innovation

The barriers to innovation comprise a familiar list of concerns. While innovation is not necessarily expensive, many managers begin with the assumption that it is. Finding a place in the budget will be difficult in the best of times, and defending the commitment to IT innovation will be even harder when times are tough.

Another inhibitor to innovation is risk aversion, and, like cost, it is often underestimated, especially by non-IT managers. IT organizations will often need to work through demonstrations and prototypes that show how risk is mitigated. Finally, it is important to weigh the consequences of not taking enough risk in a competitive environment.

Cultural norms embedded in everyday speech can form an innovation barrier. Chic Thompson (2007) provides a top ten collection of familiar innovation killers, such as *We tried that before*, *It's not in the budget*, *It's out of scope*, and the venerable preface, *Yes, but...*

In the case of IT, a significant barrier to innovation is undivided attention focused on IT operating efficiency. As we discussed earlier, enterprises need to set and revisit a balance point when allocating resources to improve operating efficiencies and cultivating innovation.

▐ In This Book ...

In designing our book, we aimed to provide the naive reader with a smooth path from basic IT business value concepts to the intricacies of building an IT innovation program. While experienced readers may choose to sample, here is our primary pathway.

Business Value Management

The foundation to our thinking about IT is that its success should be measured in business value terms. A full discussion of our thinking is in Curley (2004) and this chapter provides a nutshell explanation.

IT Innovation

IT and innovation are separate disciplines that intersect. In this chapter we share our basic strategies when managing innovative IT projects. A case study illustrates each of the six key vectors, which we believe are best managed concurrently, not sequentially.

Systemic Innovation

We believe that innovation should be pervasive in enterprises and that growth over time is well described by a capability maturity framework. This chapter identifies four components of IT innovation management, provides growth curves for each component, and describes the sequence of capabilities that emerge at each maturity level.

Innovation Capability

Our innovation capability chapter describes our ideas infrastructure and identifies the tools and methods we use at different stages in the IT innovation process. The survey is not exhaustive, but rather provides a sample that we have found useful.

Innovative Assessment

We created an innovation assessment method at Intel. It is used by teams within the IT organization and across the enterprise. We once again use a capability maturity framework to describe the increasing competence of a single team or a sampling from a larger organization. Appendix B provides additional details and stands as a model that could be tailored to fit the needs of other companies. At Intel, innovation assessment leads to explicitly-stated goals that are a part of both an organizational action plan and an individual employee's performance appraisal.

Innovation Pipeline Management

We manage innovative IT projects with the same pipeline that oversees traditional projects, but we use different criteria to make decisions. For example, while traditional systems progress at a predictable rate, innovative IT projects explore new ideas and occasionally encounter difficult obstacles. We are willing to selectively speed up and slow down projects in our innovation portfolio.

Diffusion of IT Innovation

Accelerating the adoption of new IT capabilities is one of our key principles of innovation management. While historically, diffusion was described as a social process, we push our capabilities by marketing them actively. In some cases, innovations can be wrapped into the IT refresh process and move rapidly through the company.

Launching Systemic IT Innovation

The last chapter brings together all the themes in our book and lays out a plan for building an innovation program in the IT organization. Much of the innovation activity will result in better IT systems for the company. Some of the innovation activity will support innovation excellence across the company.

Appendix A: Case Studies in IT Innovation

Two case studies are in Appendix A. One explores public sector innovation at the City of Westminster and the other traces the path of Intel's work in automating IT support whenever possible. These case studies are written in the style of a business school case and are based on interviews with the innovators to understand the challenges they faced and their strategies for success.

Appendix B: Innovation Assessment Tools

Appendix B contains a modified version of Intel's innovation self-assessment instrument and an example of how to incorporate innovation capability maturity into individual performance appraisals.

Summary

This chapter defines some of our innovation terminology and sets a direction for the remainder of the book. We have enjoyed these past years developing innovative IT systems and creating innovation capabilities for all of Intel. We believe that the combination of IT and innovation is a powerful one that is capable of transforming a company in a multitude of different ways.

Chapter 2

Business Value Management

Research turns capital into knowledge; innovation turns knowledge into capital.
—Author Unknown

Information technology and business value were once concepts quite independent of each other. Separated by terminology and organizational lines, IT and business value managers often appeared to be at odds with each other. Investments in IT cost money and the IT cost center had no charter to think in terms of profit or a return on investment.

The IT strategy was to be as operationally efficient as possible, thus minimizing cost while providing for enterprise computing needs. And IT spoke the language of availability, backup-and-restore, multi-tier architectures, and so on. Business and finance managers viewed IT as a cost of goods sold (COGS), that second entry on the income statement that subtracts away from revenue and shrinks bottom-line profit. Rather than seeking an optimum IT spend, finance often looked for a minimum level of funding.

This state of affairs began to shift as IT systems were ever more deeply integrated with critical enterprise business processes. Innovative IT systems can and do deliver increases in market share and improvements in profitability. IT and business value go hand-in-hand.

The Importance of a Common Language

The importance of a common language cannot be overstated. In order to achieve a common understanding, IT professionals need to learn more about finance, and business managers need to learn more about IT's capabilities. Company executives constitute a third community with different concerns, as shown in Figure 2.1.

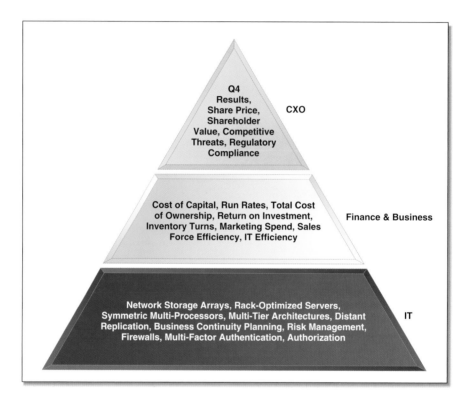

Figure 2.1 Terminology in the Enterprise: A Layered Architecture

Source: Intel IT

■ IT professionals were trained to understand information technologies such as a multi-tier architectures and symmetric multi-processors. In fact, understanding IT terms and technologies is absolutely critical to engineering agile IT infrastructure and delivering reliable IT capability.

■ Business and finance professionals talk about returns on investments, total cost of ownership, and opportunity costs. Thoughtful financial analyses are crucial to monitoring the organization's planning and execution processes.

■ Executives are strategists who should not focus on the minutiae of operations, but rather look outward at the competitive landscape. CXOs need highly condensed information from business, finance, and IT.

The Cost of Miscommunication

The downstream consequences of deferred investments present an unfortunately common example of the risks of miscommunication. IT analysts have long been aware of the lifecycle for IT system replacement and maintenance costs. Early on, systems are more reliable and their performance is at or near state of the art. Over time (measured in months, not years) systems begin to lag behind newer technologies that offer lower price/performance ratios. Moreover, maintenance costs begin to grow, software needs to be upgraded, and support for new types of storage or networking must be added.

To refresh too early is not cost effective, as finance and IT agree. To defer investment and maintain the status quo sounds ideal to the finance officer, but IT can see the vicious cycle that occurs when systems are maintained beyond their useful life. Rising maintenance costs tie up funds that could have been invested in innovative new systems. Service levels for aging systems may falter as well, leading to opportunity costs. The reputation of the IT organization can be tarnished by users who do not have the responsive systems that they expect IT to provide. Competitors with better systems can edge ahead and erode the enterprise customer base.

It is critical that the IT organization succeed in communicating this scenario to finance and business managers. When we explain these concerns, we contrast the vicious circle that deferred spending can trigger with a virtuous circle, underpinned by a spending plan communicated to finance as shown in Figure 2.2 and Figure 2.3.

Figure 2.2 shows how a modest investment in innovative IT systems that improve IT services can lead to reductions in maintenance costs. In the next budget cycle, additional resources are available to launch additional improvements and, as time goes on, cost-avoidance continues to free up funds for innovative IT systems. Figure 2.3 applies time value of money concepts to the same IT spending model. As time passes, the incremental value, in net-present-value dollars, grows sharply due to the discounting of net future value.

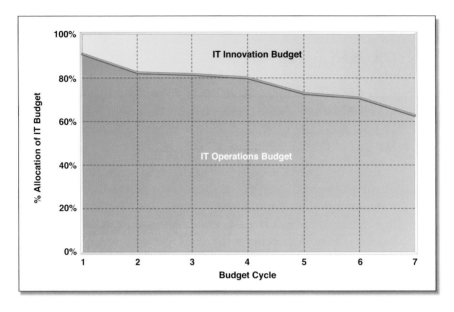

Figure 2.2 Growing the IT Innovation Budget

Source: Intel IT

Generally speaking, when IT strategists approach business and finance managers, they need to speak in terms commonly used by their audience.

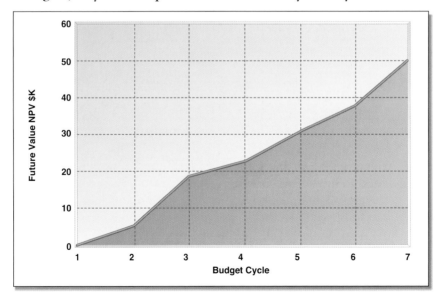

Figure 2.3 Cumulative Value in Net Present Value (NPV) Dollars

Source: Intel IT

In this case, the key terms are *dollars* and *compounding investments* leading to *business value*. The wrong terms would be *system availability* and *response time* improvements leading to a more *state-of-the-art IT solution.*

Business Value Dials

Business value dials are metrics that measure improvements and successes for the enterprise. Figure 2.4 provides examples of dials shown symbolizing their purpose as gauges. These metrics are common-language terms for financial and business planners. Inventory turns, for example, the time it takes for a complete rotation of products in inventory, is a solid standard across most industries.

The term *value dial* was coined at Intel and a library of dials has been developed over the years. The authoritative presentation of the Intel business value dial library is found in Sward (2006). David Sward provides a typology of value dials (e.g., expense avoidance dials, revenue dials), tables of examples, and sample calculations. He also provides advice

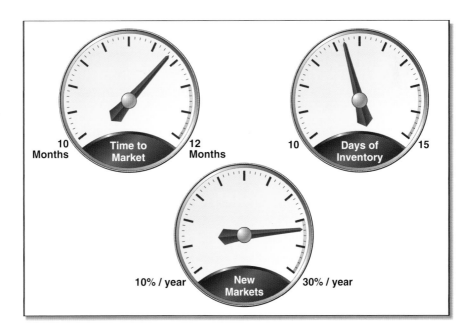

Figure 2.4 Intel's Business Value Dials

Source: Intel IT

Time Value of Money in a Nutshell

Financial analysts factor in the time value of money (TVM) when projecting initial investments, operating expenses, and returns over time. Innovative IT professionals should be comfortable with the basic concepts.

1. Which is more valuable, $100 today or $100 in five years time? Setting aside risk, $100 present value is more valuable in five years time because, had the money been banked at a 5% annual compounded rate of return, the future value would be $128. That's why we as individuals keep our savings in the bank, and not in our mattresses. The four salient variables for TVM calculations are present value (PV), future value (FV), term, and rate of return. Knowing any three, we can calculate the fourth.

2. IT promises Finance to produce $100 in future value in five years time with a rate of return is 5%. What is the present value of that future return? This process is called discounting. $78 today is equivalent to $100 in five years time. The acid test, in this tiny example, is the question, "Should IT invest $90 today to generate $100 in five years time?" And the answer is "No." If IT can return $100 in five years for $50 today, then the answer is "Maybe."

3. "Maybe" is the answer because an IT investment decision is not made in isolation. There could be a better investment, an investment that is strategically necessary, or a less risky investment. Business conditions could elevate the need for one option and reduce the need for another. IT professionals need to be adept in understanding both the insights that financial analyses provide and their limitations.

It this discussion, cash flow has been set aside. At each period in an investment, both cost and value accrue. Business models that deliver value more quickly must be weighed against longer-term gains when cash-flow concepts are integrated into the TVM calculations. Net present value (NPV) and net future value (NFV) are calculations that take cash flow into account.

Lastly, financial analysts often solve for rate of return with estimates of NPV, NFV, and term. This calculation provides a metric for both ranking investment opportunities and setting a threshold, often called a hurdle rate, for investments that make good sense from a financial analysis perspective.

All of these techniques are helpful, but they represent a single dimension. Managing by spreadsheet is a risky approach. Integrating financial analyses with other business value indicators (e.g., reputational risk, market share growth) is a good approach, in our experience.

about how to put value dials to work. A few of his top-level heuristics are as follows:

■ Formulate, standardize, and hold firmly to the measurement definitions of value dials so that you can make year-over-year and project-versus-project comparisons using the same metric.

■ Remember the importance of a baseline measure before diffusing new IT systems. A single value dial measurement after making a change provides little or no information for decision makers.

■ Favor value dials that can be transformed into dollar values. Investment decisions are best informed by costs in dollars, benefits in dollars, and an event calendar to factor in the time value of money.

Business Value and IT Efficiency

Some business managers have come to believe that gaining greater business value is at odds with gaining greater IT efficiency, and this is especially true for fielding innovative IT solutions. For those who believe that IT costs are a necessary evil, and such individuals do exist, then the best way to direct IT resources is toward efficiencies that lower operating costs while doing no harm to the organization's overall competitiveness.

Our view, to the contrary, is that business value and IT efficiency need not be at odds. In fact, there are plenty of opportunities to both improve business value contributions and increase IT efficiency. Figure 2.4 illustrates our thinking.

The framework shown in Figure 2.5 was introduced to Intel IT in the year 2000 by then-CIO Doug Busch. The framework is supported by indices that estimate the impact of an investment on IT efficiency and business value. We also estimate financial attractiveness—the level of investment needed to field each potential IT project. A portfolio of investment opportunities can be plotted within this framework, and the best investments are those landing in the cells in the upper right corner. Investments on the diagonal may make sense as well. Here are some examples of better and best investments.

■ Upgrading servers or consolidating server and storage systems may not contribute to business value, but is quite likely to improve IT efficiency. Infrastructure upgrades, generally, fall into the top center cell.

■ Investments that streamline inventory and supply chain management may not improve IT efficiency, but they contribute to greater

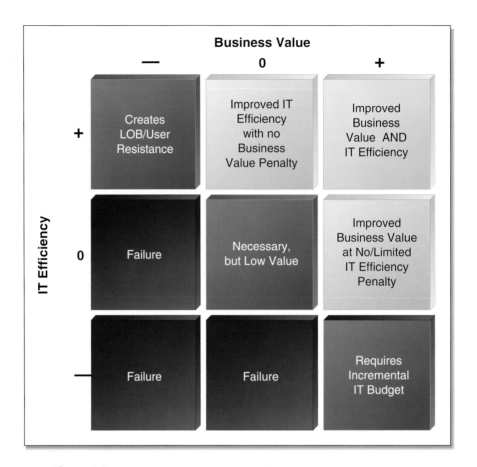

Figure 2.5 Business Value versus IT Efficiency

Source: Intel IT

business value by expediting the movement of goods for the enterprise.

■ The most desirable investments are those that improve both indicators. Examples include investments in wireless connectivity. IT efficiencies are gained since IT staff need not maintain wireline services, which ordinarily requires direct visits to the user's workspace. Business value is gained due to increased productivity for IT's customers. See Sward (2006) for a detailed discussion of the impact of mobile computing on employee productivity.

Building Innovation Business Cases

Innovation business cases often need to be considered at both a micro and macro level. If an IT innovation occurs within the boundary of a firm, then a micro business case will work. However, if the IT innovation diffuses across the firm's boundaries and into a business ecosystem or into a broader part of society, then a macro business case is needed..

For an IT innovation (or any other type of innovation) to be sustainable, the economics of the business case must be viable for both the producer and the consumer. Consumers purchase products and services when value is greater than price. Producers make products and deliver services when price is greater than cost.

Business cases for innovative IT systems deployed within the firm are simpler to prepare. The IT organization can identify and estimate costs and the population of consumers is both well known and captive. Business value dials and other measures of value can be brought into play. Thus, the necessary ingredients are available to estimate both investment and the return on investment.

For an IT innovation that cuts across an ecosystem or one that will require societal adoption, the business case will be more complex. IT planners can estimate the cost of creating an innovative product or service. Other costs, particularly distribution costs, are harder to assess. The expected value of an IT innovation used internally can be estimated, but the diffusion rate outside the firm is the most difficult estimate of all. Generally, if both aspects are value positive, that is to say that both internal and external consumers will perceive value greater than price, then the IT innovation is a "win-win," and the likelihood that the innovation will be successful and sustainable is greater.

IT Innovation Business Cases

As defined by Peppard and Tiernan (2005), four components of a business case need to be considered to fully comprehend both business and IT benefits and costs. These four components come together to estimate the return on investment (ROI). If we consider the output of an IT innovation process as a service, then the four business case components are as follows:

- BB — Business Benefits represent the value that will accrue to the business. This could include IT benefits such as improved headcount efficiency due to a server consolidation, for example.

Business benefits are also measured by value dials such as improved profitability or productivity.

■ SRC — Service Running Costs are the ongoing costs associated with providing the IT service. It is important to note that the SRC will likely exceed the original investment required to create the service. Gartner and other IT research organizations report that for each dollar spent on the original investment, up to five dollars might be spent over the lifetime to maintain and support the software.

■ SCI — The Service Creation Investment includes all the infrastructure, software acquisition, development and integration costs needed to bring the IT service into being. This is sometimes mistakenly viewed as the total cost of the project when computing ROI, which is unfortunate.

■ BCI — The Business Change Investment is the cost of preparing IT's customers to use the new service offering. Elements of cost include the development and delivery of training courses, the time that employees are away from their jobs to learn about the service, and the lower efficiency experienced until users are familiar with the service.

According to Peppard and Tiernan, these three categories of cost are mutually exclusive and exhaustive, and all are necessary to compute the return on investment. Typically, ROIs are reported for a specified length of time, which varies in different companies. Standardization within a company is useful when comparing ROI estimates for several competing projects. At Intel, we typically compute ROI for a three-year period.

The cost of the IT investment is the sum of SCI and BCI. The net return on investment is the value delivered (BB) minus the ongoing cost of running the service (SCR). The ratio of net benefit to total investment is ordinarily multiplied by 100 to express ROI as a percentage. The equation is as follows.

$$\% \, ROI \, = \, \frac{BB - SRC}{SCI + BCI} \times 100$$

ROI estimates are used in several different ways.

■ Taken alone, an ROI calculation could be a negative number, and that simply means that, as planned, the investment should not be made. In the case of IT solutions, IT innovators may need to return to the drawing board. Or, perhaps over time, technology costs will be reduced.

■ When comparing investment opportunities, ROI provides a way to rank projects. Note that ROI is unlikely to be the solitary ranking for a portfolio of innovative IT applications. The company's strategic plan, for example, may elevate an investment with a lower return.

■ The ROI estimate can also be compared to the company's hurdle rate. The hurdle rate is the threshold return on investment that is acceptable to the company. If the return is sufficiently high, then the project is fundable.

Articulation of the business case in this manner ensures both business and IT managers have a shared, comprehensive understanding of the business benefits and costs associated with the innovation. Refer to Curley (2004) and Sward (2006) for use of other multidimensional measures of business value which are important to consider in choosing a particular investment. In particular, internal rate of return, the payback period, and profitability index are useful.

Portfolio Management

Often the overall IT budget and the IT innovation budget are constrained. The objective of portfolio management is to create the highest level of return within funding constraints available. These funding constraints will be determined by both the IT and business budgets available. As a general rule having a project co-funded by both IT and the Business significantly increases the probability of success of a particular IT innovation as both organizations have skin in the gain and risk/return possibilities. Having a senior business sponsor associated with a particular innovation will substantially increase the possibility of success, as such a person can calmly quiet the naysayers or corporate antibodies that consistently try to quench interest in innovation.

Rapid iteration of the business case is essential as rapid solution prototyping and proof of concept tests are performed. The quality and reliability of financial information in the business case will be increasingly more reliable and precise if this process is followed.

Post-Implementation Review

A key factor in the success of a particular IT innovation is to perform PIRs on each innovation to determine whether the value promised was actually delivered. Doing this will substantially increase the probability that benefits will be delivered. If business conditions change, the innovation team may have to be creative and change course midstream to deliver the benefits, but having a specific target is much better than having an open-ended innovation proposition that starts with "Let's see what happens..."

To maintain balance, management needs to recognize that not all IT innovations will be successful. In IT innovation failures, it is important to fail fast and learn fast so we can quickly determine which roads we should not follow toward a particular solution.

Finally, as IT innovation becomes more predictable, a next step in maturity is to build the benefits promised in a business case into the following year's business and IT financial plans. This step can significantly increase the pressure to meet performance expectations and leads to more predictable, controllable, and sustainable innovation.

Summary

This chapter highlighted the importance of clear communication between the IT organization and finance. We looked at ways to carve out a budget for IT innovation and provided a nutshell explanation for the time value of money. We explained return on investment (ROI), a term used with different meanings across the IT industry.

We introduced our concept of business dials, which are the metrics we use to measure the return on IT investments. We took a closer look at the trade-off between IT efficiency and business value, concluding that there is a win-win potential in reviewing a portfolio of choices. We ended with a discussion of portfolio management and post-implementation reviews. For a more detailed review of business value concepts, see Curley (2004).

Chapter 3

IT Innovation

An innovation, to grow organically from within, has to be based on an
intact tradition.
—Yo Yo Ma

IT innovation is a new management discipline. It lies at the intersection of two disciplines: information technology and innovation. Both of these disciplines are still relatively immature. IT is a volatile management domain due to the high rate of technology change. Changing technology, however, fuels the innovation process as new IT capabilities emerge, and IT can act as an innovation resource, a catalyst for enabling innovation, or as an enabling platform to manage the process of innovation.

Jim Andrew, Senior VP of Innovation at Boston Consulting Group, rightly calls information the *jet fuel* of innovation. Information technology provides the capability to digitize potential innovations, which keeps the marginal cost of replicating and diffusing the innovation very low. IT innovation offers not only the challenge of creating, modifying, or repurposing new and improved ideas, but also the opportunity for accelerated diffusion.

Shifting Intel personnel to wireless laptop computers is a good example. We studied workgroup behavior, ran experiments to make sure that the laptop environment matched users' needs, and developed a business case. We identified the business dials that measured business value contributions. Finally, with support from finance and line-of-business

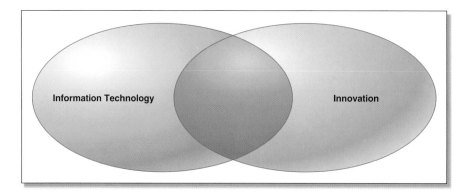

Figure 3.1 The Intersection of IT and Innovation
Source: Intel Corporation

managers, we rolled out new laptops quickly and systematically. A case study (Intel, 2003) provides a detailed account of our decision to shift to wireless laptop computing.

The Special Case of IT Innovation

IT is an unconventional resource, and it has a special relationship to innovation. Unlike most other resources consumed by enterprises, the cost of IT systems continues to drop dramatically while its performance, capacity, and flexibility continue to improve. As a result, IT provides a strong foundation for launching new and innovative solutions to enhance all types of business processes. With each passing year, returns on IT investments can increase, thus widening profit margins, not pressuring them.

IT can be a catalyst to the innovation process because managing information is itself a key part of the innovation process. For example, needs, requirements, and good ideas from IT's customers must be captured, stored, and sorted. In addition, IT infrastructure provides an accelerated method for diffusing or deploying new solutions. Overnight and around the globe, IT solutions can find their way to desktops and servers at the speed of light. When IT's customers log in with their morning tea and coffee, new features and updated information are installed and ready to go.

The marginal cost of replicating an IT innovation approximates to zero. Consider an investment in a new platform for providing support to IT customers. The yield is an improved help desk. However, the support platform can be reused to automate personnel activities for HR's customers, to assist the billing function for the enterprise's trading partners, and to perform a multitude of other support processes. (See Appendix A, eSupport at Intel.)

Finally, IT innovation can completely transform the way an organization accomplishes its objectives. In the City of Westminster, for example, policing is simply a different function when wedded with the City's extensive network of cameras. Officers can be dispatched immediately when observers see suspicious activity. The City's mobile workers can bring IT connectivity with them when conducting inspections or managing parking. (See Appendix A, Wireless Westminster.)

The Six Parallel Vectors of IT Innovation

We describe the pathway from innovation to diffusion with a set of six parallel vectors that begin with a vision and end with a measured result. On the one hand, these vectors, shown in Figure 3.2, are ordered as phases in the creation and absorption of IT innovations. At the same time, and more importantly, the vectors operate in parallel. Later phases often cause rethinking of early ones. For example, the proof-of-concept prototype is likely to change the vision of the new idea. Or, an unfavorable business case may call for additional prototyping.

Ergonomic Advising Software: Overview

At Intel, software monitors the use of the mouse by IT's customers to improve safety. Frequent mouse clicking is correlated with repetitive stress disorder. Our software can help computer users by making them aware of their mouse-clicking behavior. The application can also interrupt work to caution the customer and suggest a stretch break. Finally, data collected by the software can be mined to better understand mouse behavior for different departments and job functions.

The idea of mouse monitoring came from conversations in the corridor between an Intel safety representative and an Intel IT professional. Beginning in 2002, the project exemplifies the six vectors of innovation management in action.

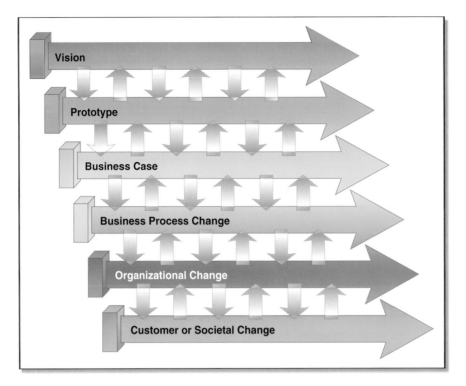

Figure 3.2 The Six Parallel Vectors of IT Innovation

Source: Intel Corporation

Vision

Most innovations actually come from a stated need or opportunity. We have all heard the generally accepted axiom of innovation, "Necessity is the mother of invention." At the same time, some of the most powerful innovations are conceptualized and motivated by compelling visions.

Consider the case of the transformation of the City of Westminster shown in Appendix A. CEO Peter Rogers had a vision of how the city could be transformed through the use of wireless technology. In Rogers's vision, city employees could spend more time on the streets providing safety and services to the City's residents, businesses, and visitors. While being more productive, these employees also could potentially be provided with better quality of life, enabling working from home, etc. A BHAG (i.e., a big hairy audacious goal) can often create the momentum, enthusiasm and energy needed to mobilize resources and people to work together to develop and realize an innovation.

However, not all innovations are as earth shattering as Wireless Westminster. Ordinarily, incremental innovations are enabled and motivated through incremental visions of how a particular task might be performed more quickly, how a particular product might perform better, or how that product could be produced more cheaply. In all cases, however, innovations are created in two phases. First is the intellectual creation manifested in the vision; next comes the physical implementation.

When the timing is right and the vision is clear, innovations can spring into life, diffuse rapidly, and quickly realize significant benefits. Thus, the first vector is aimed at creating a vision of solving a problem or taking advantage of a particular opportunity. Or, in the words of Robert Kennedy, "There are those that look at things the way they are, and ask why? I dream of things that never were, and ask why not?"

Using the lens of Keeley's ten types of innovation, a vision may be focused either on just one type or on multiple types of innovation. For example, a vision could focus narrowly on an innovative way to improve customers' experience, or a vision could aim to transform customers' experience, while also changing the business model.

For example, the Walt Disney Company introduced a Photopass system enabling after-the-fact purchase of photos taken at Disney theme parks. Professional photographers roam the park snapping pictures, which are immediately available or available later on a Web site. This innovation changed the user experience for visitors and also changed the business model. A Disney visitor could continue to purchase products from Disney days after the visit was over. Photopass created improved customer service and enhanced revenue streams for Disney. Continuous experimentation and prototyping was a hallmark of making this particular IT innovation work. Early prototypes were not immediately successful.

Thus, the first vector is aimed at creating a vision of a better way to perform a business process with an IT capability. The vision should be user centered and describe how a business process could be better accomplished. Tracking down problematic processes and observing the people who perform the work are common ethnographic methods for drawing out process requirements and understanding where potential technology solutions might be applied. (See Chapter 5 for a discussion of ethnographic research.)

To move an innovation from the vision to the prototype stage, it is important to clearly communicate the vision to gain buy-in from management and to ensure that the vision is shared by the team that is expected to make it successful.

Ergonomic Advising Software: Vision

Repetitive motion injuries related to use of the mouse were appearing in the Intel safety organization's database and researchers were reporting a linkage to the frequency of mouse clicks and the duration of uninterrupted work.

Meanwhile, in the year 2000, a shareware program called Mouse-Count was published by KittyFeet Software and was being used by a small number of IT customers in Intel. MouseCount monitored users' mouse click behavior and wrote raw data to files each day, month, and year. The inventor envisioned MouseCount as a platform for a contest for the *most* clicks.

These two unrelated events triggered the idea of building an ergonomic monitoring system to an Intel safety officer at Ireland Fab Operations, Tom Mooney. What if software could monitor the behavior of computer users and measure the risk due to overwork with the mouse? What if safety engineers could study usage in different communities to see which job categories were at greater risk? And, finally, what if the software could warn users and suggest that they take a break from mousing?

At this point in the process, the safety engineer has recognized a problem, an opportunity, and a reapplication of an existing innovation to a new usage. Namely, repetitive motion can cause injury, we can identify those at risk and warn people, and the idea of counting mouse clicks can be put to use as an early warning system. In the end, the ergonomic advising software turned out to be 20% invention and 80% reapplication.

From Vision to Prototype

Visions are best communicated by example. A prototype is a small-scale solution that certifies that the IT solution is viable. Prototypes also demonstrate the vision to stakeholders and provide a test bed for making improvements based on new ideas and potential concerns. Prototypes are also useful for estimating how much a business process can be improved and thus what the business value contribution is likely to be.

A prototype in the hands of a user is invaluable for deciding if the innovation will be able to meet its intended function and use.

Ergonomic Advising Software: Prototype

MouseCount provided a simple platform for initial experiments prior to prototyping. Tom approached Brendan Cannon of the IT Innovation Centre with some of the early MouseCount usage data, passed on some suggestions on how the product could be improved, and the two speculated on the potential for an expanded application. Intel IT collected data for 27 weeks from 26 volunteers. These raw data not only highlighted the high rate of mouse clicking, but also helped to identify additional functionality that was needed. Daily counts, for example, was too coarse a grain size. To provide preemptive advice to the user, hourly measures are needed.

Manual analysis of the data, while acceptable during this experimental stage and, in fact, attractive to the engineering mind, would need to be automated to make the system practical and efficient for a broader base of users. Similarly, a production system would need a central repository for the data to support studies of variances within and among departments, job categories, and applications. And, based on conversations with IT customers, the issue of privacy emerged as important.

To be accepted, the prototyping team reasoned, employees must feel comfortable sharing these data. And, Intel has explicit policies about protecting employee privacy. This thinking led the Intel team to include the capability for employees to choose anonymity when reporting data to the central database.

Prototypes vary in sophistication. Simple prototypes can be developed during a workshop to communicate a vision and gain buy-in for further exploration of an innovation's potential. More complex prototypes require buy-in from management to allocate the resources. As highlighted by the ergonomic monitoring prototype, it is crucial to build a prototype with which to test the scope and the requirements of a finished product.

Many IT technologists believe that the hard part of innovation is building the technology solution. It is difficult to wrestle with complexity and sometimes there is significant technical risk. However, in our experience with IT innovations, solving technical problems is very often the easy part. Soft factors such as business process and organizational change often emerge as the most difficult. Joint accountability between the business and IT is essential for the successful development and adoption of an IT-based innovation.

When an IT innovation is realized, the prototype is ready to be converted into a product and is often offered as an service. We think in terms of the principles articulated in Geoffrey Moore's *Crossing the Chasm* (1991/1999). Early adopters are happy to exercise a prototype, which may have intricacies and incompleteness. To aim for the early majority, however, means building a complete product that fits into the user's experience as comfortably as possible.

Thus, when a new IT service can reuse existing user interfaces or the look-and-feel of familiar services, the barrier to successful adoption will be significantly lowered. Moreover, when a new IT service can use an existing architecture and reuse code modules, the cost of both development and maintenance can be substantially reduced.

The disciplines and skills of prototyping are not the same as those needed to engineer production systems. Also, while a prototype is an important step forward, it is but the second step on the path to delivering business value. The third step is building the business case.

Business Case

We believe that the importance of building a business case is illustrated by the wide swings in IT investment over the past decade. Before the dotcom crash, many IT innovations were funded due to irrational optimism fueled by the disruptive adoption of the Internet and the compelling need to remain competitive in a changing world. In other words, no business case was required.

This was followed by a period of irrational pessimism where many IT business cases were rejected out of hand due to the bad experience in the dotcom crash or the unavailability of capital for further IT investments. Over-investment in Internet-enabled innovations combined with investments made to mitigate Year 2000 risk brought many businesses to the point of having neither time nor capital to invest.

We are happy to report that, by 2007, a modicum of balance has been regained. Good IT investments with strong business cases are often reviewed with objectivity and many are approved. One legacy of the wild swings of irrational optimism and pessimism is that few innovations are funded without a strong business case. And this is as it should be: the presence of a credible and compelling business case substantially increases the probability of a successful innovation and the associated conversion of value potential into value creation.

Business Cases, Prototypes, and Vision

Typically, for an innovation to be viable and sustainable, a return on investment (ROI) needs to be created for the producer's costs, operating costs, and the consumer's benefits. In the early stages of an innovation project, some form of valuation is necessary to justify and sustain the investment. At the vision stage, it is difficult to estimate value with any precision, and methodologies such as using a business value index (Curley 2004) can be useful. A pro-forma business case is also useful.

As the innovation journeys through the product lifecycle pipeline, more information becomes available. We review and refine our business cases regularly. We also use rapid solution prototyping in conjunction with real-time business case iteration to produce business cases with improved confidence and precision in a few weeks time. Decision makers tracking innovative IT projects can look at the work in progress and re-estimate costs and business value contributions.

Note that the prototype and business case should confirm or refine the vision. It is not uncommon for adjustments to be made, and this is a good place in the pipeline process for a stage gate.

Moreover, often the decision to invest in an innovative IT solution is a differential one. Among a collection of choices, and taking into account the available budget, we must choose the best candidates.

Go, No Go

Decision makers, informed by business cases, launch or stall innovative IT projects. When launched, the IT development organization hardens the prototype, expands it to be complete, tests it repeatedly, and integrates it with other IT systems. If we are successful, then an innovative IT project and a conventional IT project will both be well managed. We want to identify and mitigate technical risks in the prototyping phase when sunk costs remain small. When the decision is *go*, we aim to deliver on time, on budget, and on specification.

Stage Gates

Stage gating divides the product innovation process into stages—typically five or six. Between the stages are virtual gates (often meetings) that act as checkpoints at which the gate can be opened or closed for a project to move to the next stage.

Business Process Change

> ### Ergonomic Advising Software: Business Case
>
> When Intel can invest a few thousand dollars to improve employee safety, they will do it every time and in an instant. Intel IT innovators explained their vision to different groups and folded statements of support from a broad constituency into their business plan.
>
> Prototyping had expanded their vision. The ergonomic monitoring system could provide data useful to the software development community. Some software applications require more mouse clicks than others. Software developers could use these data to reconsider the design of their user interfaces.
>
> Moreover, when evaluated as potential intellectual property, the ergonomic monitoring system qualified and Intel IT initiated the patent process. Intel IT deferred the decision of whether to build and sell such a product or to license others to do so.

When innovative IT solutions roll out, they inevitably cause changes in business processes. Process owners will need to endorse these changes and training is often required for staff members who will re-engage work in a different way.

For some innovations, the switch-over from old methods to new ones can be quite complex. Old and new systems may need to co-exist for a period of time until process owners gain confidence in the new solution. Adoption of business change will often require a change manager who actively attends to the change process. This is another case where the technology solution may have been difficult to achieve, but the acceptance of changes in business processes may be even harder for IT's customers. And, ironically, the more perceived benefits associated with a particular innovation, the more likely the business process change is to be adopted.

Organizational Change

Many IT innovations require organizational changes in order to realize value. If an organization is unwilling to change, or is already exhausted from trying to assimilate too many other innovations, then failure is likely. Most organizations have a certain tolerance for change, and the wise IT strategist keeps this rate in mind.

Ergonomic Advising Software: Business Process Change

The ergonomic software was offered on a voluntary basis to Intel IT's customers and it diffused throughout the Intel Ireland community quite quickly. One of the first findings when mining the centralized database was seasonality. Not surprisingly, when budgets were about to be set, financial analysts were clicking at a ferocious rate. Safety officers learned when and where to sound alerts.

IT customers reported that they were more aware of their mouse behavior and that they were proactively looking for alternatives. In many cases, a computer user can choose a keyboard shortcut in place of a mouse click or modify toolbar choices to make two-click operations into one-click operations. And, most importantly, a stretch break is needed when click frequencies exceed thresholds of safety.

IT and business people alike will resist the adoption of innovation if it puts their job at risk or if it substantially changes their work-life balance or working conditions. Creating win-win scenarios can be very helpful in ensuring that organizational change comes about through commitment rather than compliance.

Innovative IT solutions can also instigate change to the IT organization. For example, when Intel IT's *People, Intellectual Capital, and Solutions Group* realized that we were one of the largest consumers of IT solutions, we realized that we were uniquely suited to document what we had learned and to share this knowledge with fellow IT travelers.

We brought in writers and editors to work with IT subject-matter experts to produce white papers on best known methods. The project grew from a single idea until it reached a critical mass that led to the formation a new dedicated group called IT@Intel.

Customer or Societal Change

Because we define innovation as the adoption of something new which creates value, this final vector of customer adoption is critically important. As information technology becomes more and more pervasive, IT innovations touch many aspects of society. For any innovation to be adopted, it has to meet at least three primary criteria:

- Utility—The solution solves a real problem.
- Ease of use—The solution is appealing to the customer.

Ergonomic Advising Software: Organizational Change

In the case of office ergonomics, IT and Safety formed a team to explore Tom Mooney's bright idea. While organizational change often refers to large-scale adjustments, partnerships like this one reflect organizational teamwork that is critical to the success of most IT innovations. IT and Marketing, IT and Engineering, IT and Finance, and a host of other partnerships are necessary.

The ergonomic monitoring system radically changed the tasks performed by Intel's office ergonomics teams. Rather than observing work with ethnographic techniques, these professionals could now study a journal of events captured in a database. And, the monitoring system provided a platform capable of capturing additional events as needed. The ergonomic advising software became a general-purpose instrument panel focused on individual behavior when using a personal computer.

■ Business benefit—The company delivers shareholder value.

A producer must be willing to invest in the innovation, customers or users must be willing to pay for the innovation, and business value benefit must accrue. These are the hard-line facts about IT innovation in business.

The Public Sector

We speak in business value terms because that is the context of our direct experience. We recognize that there are other contexts, particularly public sector organizations. For those who seek to provide the best possible services to their customers on a non-profit basis, most of these same principles apply.

The concepts of cost and return on investment (ROI) remain firmly in place. The goal of cost avoidance remains the same. Why spend more when efficiencies allow a non-profit to spend less? Market share applies as well—a successful non-profit can afford to reach out more widely. Customer satisfaction remains in place.

The slippery slope for the public sector is the absence of a profit metric. In business, we expect dollars returned for our investments. In the case of the public sector, the profit metric is replaced by quality of service, reduction of risk, and measures that show quality-of-life improvements for customers served. The non-profit public-sector organization can be run like a business, and we recommend this approach. See the case study on Wireless Westminster in Appendix A.

Customer Sensitivities

IT innovations can be threatening to IT's customers. Customers and users must come to believe that the benefits of using the innovation are greater than the downside risks associated with the collection of personal data. An everyday example that is increasingly common is the retail loyalty card. Shoppers use loyalty cards to qualify for discounts on goods and services, even though most know that their personal shopping patterns are being collected and analyzed.

Ergonomic Advising Software: Customer or Societal Change

The most immediate benefits of ergonomic advising software are identifying and measuring a risk to computer users. When it comes to office ergonomics, the adage *forewarned is fore-armed* takes hold. Intel IT customers are now aware that excessive mouse clicking is a risk and that it is manageable. They can measure their behavior against benchmarks, and Intel safety programs can provide mitigation strategies to reduce risk. They can target their efforts.

The ergonomic advising software is well positioned to inform the software design society as well. While Douglas Engelbart's mouse was a radical innovation, understanding its weaknesses is critical to improving the quality of software designs. Graphical user interfaces are often viewed as an art form. The ergonomic advising software provides empirical data that nudges the design effort from art to science. Measured results galvanize engineers to improve products that avoid injury.

Google Mail or Gmail is an innovative IT service that, on the face of it, has a pure advertising business model (i.e., a free lunch for users) and, in some countries, has been adopted by many consumers. However, in countries such as Germany, adoption rates are much lower due to a higher level of concern about privacy implications of IT. While Gmail may successfully satisfy the five other vectors of innovation management, the degree of alignment with all six vectors may limit its take-up and effectiveness. Time will tell.

As the diffusion process continues, we do expect to see changes in customer or society behavior. For example, at Intel we saw that the installation of sensors in conference rooms to detect motion and turn lights off after periods of no movement generating arm-waving behavior and Dilbert cartoons. Other innovations hopefully have brought more productive changes.

■ The advent of instant messaging (IM) caused people in meetings to start asking clarifying questions of other attendees without interrupting the meeting. However, for others, it creates a situation where important and urgent messages can take precedence over less important and non-urgent tasks.

Repeated interruption from IM messages and also the consumption of cpu cycles on an already overtaxed laptop mean that people often turn off instant messaging.

■ The adoption of the Blackberry wireless message system is an interesting IT innovation to watch in action. It has transformed the communication flow to and from executives creating a just-in-time or real-time workflow for business decision making.

On the downside, some users of the Blackberry find it is addictive and repeatedly check for new email messages. This causes a deflection of concentration in meetings resulting in a continuous partial attention phenomenon.

■ Wireless home networks enable employees to do work at home while watching TV or even in bed. We do not want to explore this vein of innovative, pervasive IT.

The biggest reward for innovators is often the opportunity to observe the changes their vision in action has made in the lives of their customers, or even in society as a whole. For example, the creators of our ergonomic advising software know that they are contributing to making their colleagues' lives better by helping prevent injury.

Innovation and Societal Change in India

An example from Intel's India Innovation Centre is the use of web cameras for telemedicine. Rural India has scarce access to medical experts. Because medical examination and diagnosis often requires days of travel, web cameras are now being set up to allow opticians to make preliminary examinations and determine whether it is necessary to make a trip for treatment.

Again, in India, the migration of certain government services to the Internet is allowing farmers to remain home and work their land instead of having to spend several days travelling into cities to obtain business licenses, birth and marriage certificates, and other licenses and permits. Rural PC kiosks that are making this possible are becoming part of the social fabric of the villages and gathering places for the residents.

Summary

Managing the six vectors concurrently can lead to more predictable innovation. Conversely, managing IT Innovation without concurrent re-examination of all vectors is a recipe for failure. A missing vector, such the absence of a business case, is a clear invitation for failure.

One of the biggest challenges to successful innovations and innovation leadership is resistance to change. Three of the six vectors are related to change. Along with excellent communications, understanding change management is critical to long-term success.

Chapter 4

Systemic Innovation

Systematic innovation consists in the purposeful and organized search for changes, and in the systematic analysis of the opportunities such changes might offer for economic or social innovation.
—Peter F. Drucker

Systemic innovation is the pervasive and ongoing search for new ideas that improve business processes and deliver business value. Innovation is systemic when it becomes a way of life. In this chapter we examine the whole of systemic innovation and identify different levels of maturity and sophistication. Later chapters will look into facets of systemic innovation in greater detail. Our objective here is to provide a reference model.

This is a chapter that applies both to IT innovation and to innovation in general. IT organizations that excel in managing their own innovation processes are well positioned to share that expertise with the enterprise as a whole. Demonstrated success within the IT organization is also a powerful way to gain corporate-wide respect.

Especially in the case of innovation infrastructure—the tools and methods learned, developed, and tailored to a company's industry and markets—the IT organization's experience can be highly leveraged and the investment in IT innovation can find even greater returns.

Managing Systemic Innovation

In the early days at Intel, quality, safety, and innovation shared a reputation for being unmanageable. People spoke of quality as an art that could neither be measured nor managed, and that the size of a manufacturing run should be increased to cover the inevitable number of defects. Similarly, improvements in safety were haphazard. These two functions, in turn, have been brought under methodical control. We believe that managers of systemic innovation can learn from past experiences with quality and safety management.

You Will!

In the 1980s, Intel faced competitors who began to use quality as a differentiator. According to then-CEO Craig Barrett, "When other companies began to compete on quality, then the equation changed and people's attitudes had to change."

Barrett went on to say, "We approached quality like any standard engineering problem at Intel. We found that if you defined the problem, collected data, intelligently used statistics, and made data-based decisions, you could improve the quality of any process or product."

To emphasize his commitment to quality, Barrett added the phrase, "You Will" in the margin of his presentation graphics. As Barrett put it, "[This was my] message that things had to change." And the message resounded throughout Intel.

"The rest is history," Barrett summarized some years later. "We trained the whole company on how to use statistics to make valid decisions, we implemented process controls throughout the manufacturing process, we found that we could consistently exceed our own expectations on yields and quality, and we continue to do so today."

Most companies consider that innovation is already a part of their culture, but to maintain their competitive edge, they need to foster long-term systemic innovation. Today's companies need to move beyond historically recognized—though still very important—innovation activities such as obtaining patents and developing new technology. They need to embrace less obvious innovation such as business models, process innovation and delivery innovations. A systemic innovation program enables a company to manage innovation as a culture in the same way that quality and safety have come to be managed.

Saying that quality cannot be measured and managed sounds ludicrous today. When Craig Barrett implemented quality management at Intel he provided the links between existing tools and the support required to use them, such as training and process controls. In a similar fashion, companies that have embraced an environmental health and safety culture can tell you the financial value of having a safety culture, and those that adopted a safety culture late can also tell you the cost of being behind that curve. There is risk in being behind the curve for implementing a culture of innovation. The inflection point for other companies and countries using innovation as a strategic competitive weapon has arrived.

Systematic Innovation and Systemic Innovation

When we describe innovation as systemic, we mean that the innovation capability is pervasive throughout the company and innovation is a way of life. Like quality and safety, innovation is always a part of what we do. It is woven into the company's genetic code and replicated as a rite of passage for new employees. It is celebrated and rewarded. Systemic innovation is more of an end-state and less of a roadmap. Systemic innovation is widely discussed in the innovation literature and is an increasingly used to describe innovation at Intel.

When we describe innovation as systematic, we mean that managing excellence in innovation can be a rational and methodical process. Innovation does not simply become systemic; effort, skills, and investments are required. Without careful management, innovation efforts can be ineffective. As Drucker (1986) argued, with management, innovation efforts become purposeful and measured.

We focus on both systemic and systematic innovation to provide a balanced view. Each term contributes to a comprehensive discussion.

Systemic innovation is not an art that demands unmanaged creativity, nor is it used exclusively by the research and development department. Systemic innovation is a discipline in which everyone can be engaged and involved. And it adds measurable value to the bottom line.

Systemic Innovation

We view systemic innovation as a four-stage process that operates much like a control loop. As Figure 4.1 shows, the process is ongoing and cyclical. IT innovation can be managed like a business. Strategic and tactical management decisions determine the IT innovation budget. The budget fuels the IT innovation capabilities that deliver new solutions. Then, finally, as IT innovations are diffused, they reach realization and generate business value. Like a business, managers monitor the relationship between investment and payoff as the control loop is closed.

This is a general-purpose model that applies equally well when systemically innovating a company's business models, engineering processes, and its products and services. At the same time, we shall continue to use IT innovation as our base case. In a nutshell, when the four stages in the systemic innovation control loop are mature, each stage operates as follows:

■ In the *Manage Innovation Like a Business* stage, IT and business managers set innovation strategy and allocate the budget in accordance with that strategy. They review the results of prior investments to optimize the innovation portfolio spend. On a regular basis, these stakeholders review the innovation project pipeline and adjust resources in line with progress reports on each project. They review and realign often their shifting IT requirements as the company responds to shifting markets.

■ Based on guidance from the managers of innovation investment, IT managers *Manage the Innovation Budget* in a dynamic fashion. Innovative projects may be accelerated or retarded for a variety of reasons. IT managers can also stretch the budget by working with open innovation consortia or supplement it by licensing IT innovations to other organizations.

■ The heart of the IT innovation process lies in *Manage the Innovation Capability*. This is a broad category and includes innovation infrastructure, both for the IT organization and for the enterprise at large. Innovation capability includes maintaining professional skillsets. IT systems that capture and manage suggestions and requirements from IT's customers are also a part of the innovation capability.

The tools and techniques for diffusing IT innovations are critical as well. Accelerated diffusion and adoption of solutions results in accelerated value capture. With a distributed, global infrastructure,

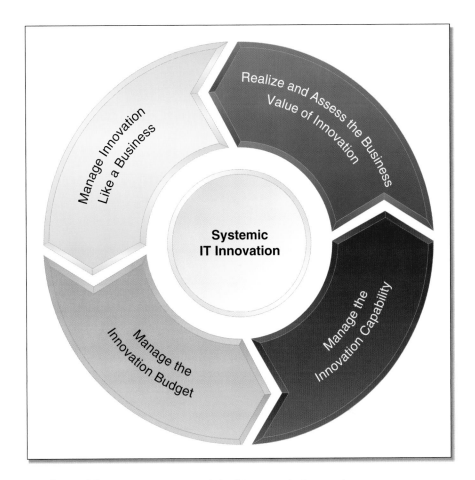

Figure 4.1 Control Loop Model of Systematic Innovation

Source: Intel IT

new IT solutions can be deployed very quickly to accelerate value creation.

■ The final stage in the control loop is *Realize and Assess the Business Value of Innovations*. In a mature IT organization, this means that the pipeline of innovations delivers real systems in a timely fashion and that those systems produce measured business benefits to the enterprise. Especially for IT, customer satisfaction is an important benefit. Other benefits include accelerating work, improving quality, and supporting collaboration.

Of particular interest is IT-led business innovation. Business value accrues when entrepreneurial leaders from the IT organization deliver new business products, services, or models.

The control loop is closed, as shown in Figure 4.1, when tools and metrics are in place to capture the information needed to *Manage IT Innovation like a Business*.

Capability Maturity Framework for Systemic Innovation

In our experience, systemic innovation capabilities are not mature when innovation programs are launched. The IT innovation capability maturity framework (CMF) shown in Table 4.1 describes the evolutionary manner in which competencies grow. The CMF breaks out critical processes from larger bundles called macro-processes. Our control loop stages become the macro-processes for the IT Innovation CMF.

Ad Hoc

In many IT organizations, efficiency and cost-effectiveness dominate the planning process. Innovative IT opportunities will arise from time to time, but they are not budgeted on a regular basis and there is no infrastructure available to support them. When IT's customers voice their needs loudly

Table 4.1 Capability Maturity Framework for Systemic Innovation

Maturity Level	Macro-processes			
	Manage Innovation Like a Business	Manage the Innovation Budget	Manage the Innovation Capability	Realize and Assess Business Value
Optimizing	Continuous realignment	Amplified budget	Innovation excellence	Predictable, probable, and profitable
Advanced	Explicit strategy	Significant co-funding	Infrastructure integrated	Proactive change management
Intermediate	Management commitment	Formal budget allocation	Infrastructure established	Active change management
Basic	Tacit tolerance	Informal budget allocation	Occasional skunk works	Informal assessment
Initial	← Ad Hoc →			

enough, the IT manager forms a team to address the issue or hires in a consultant who is a specialist in the area of concern. And, when a system is fielded and customer complaints diminish, the team is disbanded until the next customer crisis. In a nutshell, in initial maturity level shown in the bottom row of the CMF shown in Table 4.1, the IT organization is averse to innovation and the risk that it brings to everyday IT operations. This level of maturity is often called *chaos* in the management literature.

IT Innovation CMF Basic Level of Maturity

The primitive signs that innovation is maturing begin with management awareness and tacit tolerance, as shown in the basic maturity level in Table 4.1. Early innovative projects are ordinarily driven by a hero—an IT professional who takes on a challenge, fights to squeeze a few funds out of the IT budget, and brings a novel IT capability to life. There is no innovation budget, but managers are willing, from time to time, to free funds and time, often under pressure from users or business managers. Occasionally, teams are formed and the skunk works produces a result. Sometimes pet projects are funded when an idea finds a manager to champion it, but funding is based on emotion, not data. Most often, value assessment is informal, often lacking a baseline against which to measure improvement.

At the basic level there is frequently a mélange of tools and systems that are supporting the existing levels of innovation in the company. For example, there might be problem solving training, people might practice brainstorming, and the engineering community might be designing experiments and developing prototypes as part of the product development lifecycle. However, the existing tools are not components of an integrated innovation system.

It is difficult to find employee communications on the topic of innovation and an innovation strategy is lacking. And, there is often resistance from designated innovators, such as members of the research and development team to establishing an innovation system for all employees or managers. At the basic level, innovation is associated with creativity and the majority of investment in innovation is for product development.

IT Innovation CMF Intermediate Level of Maturity

The cornerstone to improving innovation capabilities is management commitment, which describes the intermediate level of maturity for the IT innovation CMF. Leaders in the company with authority and vision must decide that innovative excellence is a core competency that the company must have. For companies in the middle of a pack of competitors, an emphasis on innovation can be a break-away strategy. For companies aiming to enter a market filled with incumbent players, innovation provides differentiation. Industry leaders view innovation as a necessary competence in order to maintain market share and to create new markets.

With management support comes oversight and visibility. Ideally, the fledgling IT innovation function can work with counsel from a committee of both business and technical managers. This group provides a sounding board for new ideas and also can bring to the IT innovators problems that need to be solved to expedite the company's business processes.

Companies need to move beyond a historically recognized—though still very important—innovation focus at the basic level, such as patents and new technology, to embrace less obvious innovation such as business models, process innovation, and delivery innovations. This might also include having individuals share best practices on how to manage a project, for example, or discussions among employees about better collaboration methods.

At the intermediate level, a systemic innovation program enables a company to manage innovation as a culture in the same way that quality and safety are managed. Innovation metrics begin to appear and the IT organization starts to apply engineering discipline and marketing techniques to actively diffuse innovation throughout the organization. It is often at this level when companies realize that competitors are successfully using innovation as a strategic advantage. That realization creates a sense of urgency in management to commit to investment in innovation.

IT Innovation Budget

With management support, a formal budget allocation is established, the stage is set for methodical activities across the CMF. Over budget cycles, the innovation budget can grow if the new IT solutions improve overall IT efficiency. Efficiency gains are especially large when innovative solutions replace high-maintenance legacy systems. Cost avoidance and cost reduction often provide the greatest contribution from innovative IT systems at the intermediate level of maturity.

IT Innovation Capability

A typical first activity at the intermediate level is building infrastructure. Education and training come first. Members of the IT organization need to learn about the opportunities and risks that are characteristic of innovative application development. For many IT organization dominated by financial and enterprise resource planning (ERP) systems maintenance, new software tool and language competencies will need to develop.

Rapid solution prototyping and user-centered design concepts and methods are particularly important for innovation-oriented IT practitioners.

Managers assigned to creating innovative IT capabilities need not build and collapse their organizations, as the ad-hoc skunk works managers did. Rather, experience can accrue as a growing stream of innovative products emerges. Continuity in the creation process leads to greater efficiencies as good IT ideas fielded to one part of the company can be copied exactly or adapted to needs elsewhere in the company. Winning projects can be rewarded, whereas the reward for the skunk works team was disbandment.

The newly-formed innovation team must learn about the critical role of active diffusion when deploying innovative capabilities. When a valuable IT system is not used, it gives back no value. At this intermediate level of maturity, we would expect the IT organization to spend more time announcing new IT capabilities and explaining why IT customers should put them to use. Initially, this is often an informal process. In the early days of the ergonomic advisor project at Intel (see page 39), one manager simply went from cubicle to cubicle to demonstrate the system's capability.

Creating an innovation pipeline begins at the intermediate level. The formal budget sets a cap on the number of innovation projects that can be launched. A queue is needed and the IT organization needs to track these projects through prototyping, development, and deployment. As explained in greater depth in Chapter 7, there are advantages in blending innovative projects with traditional ones if the IT organization has an existing pipeline management methodology.

For its own purposes and for the enterprise at large, the IT organization develops idea capture and development systems. Archiving ideas from across the enterprise and from trading partners and customers outside of the enterprise is a valuable activity. These systems are often Web-based to support widespread access.

Finally, at this level the IT organization begins offering innovation training and workshops for its own staff and for others in the company. At Intel, we call these offerings innovation services.

Business Value Realized and Assessed

Active, methodical assessment processes are formalized at the intermediate level of maturity. The IT organization cultivates a collection of metrics such as the business value dials described in Chapter 2, and collecting data both before and after an innovation is introduced becomes routine. The process of change management comes into focus as experience in rolling out innovative IT solutions accumulates.

As demonstrated with our six vectors of innovation described in Chapter 3, the IT organization now knows that the realization of innovative solutions affects business processes, organizations, and ultimately the customers and culture of the company. Different metrics are needed to tap into all three of the outcome categories.

IT Innovation CMF Advanced Level of Maturity

The advanced level of IT innovation capability is marked by a shift from merely creating business value to maximizing business value. Innovation managers pay increased attention to longer-term planning and to those innovation opportunities with the best likelihood of payback. IT and business leaders look to the team for an explicit statement of strategy that provides structure, purpose, and priority to the innovation process. As the number of innovative products grows, the innovation team creates portfolios of similar projects and the pipeline management process becomes more fine grained.

Investment managers formalize measures of business value as a part of the planning process, and a business case is required for each innovation opportunity. In our experience, when innovation is valued, there are always too many good ideas. It is the task of the innovation managers to choose the best ideas and to muster resources in accordance with cost, benefit, and risk. Also, in our experience, when innovative IT opportunities are evaluated in this way, priorities are not hard to set and contention among those arguing merely for the cleverness of a new idea is quelled. The systemic innovation process rests on a rational business foundation.

IT Innovation Budget

At the advanced level of maturity, IT innovation managers begin to find ways to defend a growing budget. Demonstrated business value over several budget cycles provides the foundation, of course. At this level, IT innovation managers are keenly aware that they are competing for each investment dollar. Should the enterprise spend more on manufacturing technologies, product marketing efforts, or an IT innovation? The decision is differential, and the IT innovators must differentiate themselves in order to succeed.

Co-funding is another way to leverage the IT innovation budget. A compelling customer care prototype just might trigger investment from the sales department, for example. An innovative forecasting application developed for the finance department may be attractive to the strategic marketing group, especially since a second deployment will be less costly. And, in many corners of the world, funds for innovation and training are available from government agencies, labor unions, and other stake-holders. The European Sixth Framework is one example; the US state of California's training grant program is another.

Stakeholder commitment to IT innovation grows as the IT systems for cultivating enterprise-wide innovation emerge. Investments in IT can directly transform an enterprise to be far more innovative. The reputation of the enterprise is enhanced when customers and trading partners can see visible support for innovation. Enterprises that are adept at innovation create products and services that open new markets and reach out to new customers. When IT delivers robust support to the enterprise, potential gains in business value are enormous.

IT Innovation Capability

An integrated infrastructure is the trademark of an advanced level of inno-vation capability. Workshops, assessment techniques, and skillsets form a pipeline, not for projects, but for IT and business professionals. IT courseware and workshops bring newly hired employees systematically into the culture of innovation.

From their PC desktop, IT customers can look in on new and emerging innovative systems. Google provides Google Labs to fill this function. Visi-tors can exercise prototype and early development applications to see what is coming next. Not only does early access whet the appetite for IT's customers, it also provides feedback and comments that can be invaluable to the system designers and developers.

Moreover, user-centered innovation directs the prototyping process. At this level of maturity, the IT organization has a well-developed under-standing of the different audiences that it serves. Customers are directly involved in innovative system development.

Guided by IT management and budget allocation, IT innovation managers align their work with enterprise goals and objectives. Major innovations such as executing improved supply chain management always have an equally major business sponsor. The melding of business and technical expertise in support of innovation is key to success at this level of maturity.

Creating innovative capabilities is user-centered at the advanced matu-rity level. The kernel of user-centered design is equality between developer and user. In prior levels of maturity, users were involved, but in the extreme, the IT organization imposed its solution on its customers.

At the advanced level, IT innovators are concerned with collections of *user interactions* that make up the entire *user experience*. Help-desk personnel can use IT systems to expedite their work, as shown in the case study on Innovative eSupport at Intel, Part 1 on page 172. However, it is important for innovators to understand the entire context in which this work is embedded.

In addition to running campaigns to push IT innovations toward IT's customers, in the advanced maturity level, diffusion managers begin to use technology itself. In some cases, innovations can be bundled with new platforms when hardware refreshment occurs. Many innovations are invisible and simply assist users behind the scenes. Others can be offered as a part of the operating system image and do not need to be downloaded from a Web site. Technology-based push is one of the reasons why IT innovation can diffuse very rapidly. Moving an innovation to user desktops in an internetworked world can happen in seconds.

Business Value Realized and Assessed

Proactive change management marks the advanced level of maturity for realizing and assessing innovative IT solutions. Streamlined distribution channels accelerate innovations into widespread usage and the assessment process gains sophistication as well. IT organizations at this level address the challenges of converting soft benefits into dollar terms.

One category of traditionally soft benefits is improvements in productivity. Controlled experiments can measure time spent on typical tasks for existing and proposed IT solutions. These experiments generate estimates of time saved, and employee time can be transformed into monetary units (Sward 2007).

IT Innovation CMF Optimizing Level of Maturity

Notice that this level of maturity is called *optimizing* and not optimized. Here and in other writing (Curley 2004), we contend that IT organizations do not become mature; rather, they reach a high level of performance and then improvement becomes incremental and continuous. The increments will be smaller; the large improvements occur between lower levels of maturity, to be sure. However, marginal returns can be higher due to reuse of innovations and the amortization of infrastructure costs over many innovation projects.

Changes in the enterprise goals and objectives combined with improvements in information technologies demand a continuous monitoring of the alignment of IT innovations with business needs. The concept car built three years ago may be ready for daily use at a reasonable price point, for example. Competitive pressure may elevate the priority of innovations aimed at reducing time to market. Thus, even the best-managed innovation organization will experience constant change, and adjustments will be necessary in order to maximize returns.

IT Innovation Budget

An amplified budget is one where the IT organization begins to generate a revenue stream from outside the enterprise. This is accomplished primarily by licensing the IT organization's intellectual property. IT innovations can be productized and marketed more effectively by third parties in most cases.

Participating in open innovation consortia is another way to amplify the IT innovation budget. This approach is not primarily a cost-avoidance strategy aimed at lowering the investment in R&D by sharing costs with others. Rather, open innovation consortia often deliver higher quality results more quickly that a single company's efforts. Intel IT participates in Disorient, at *www.itsharenet.org*, where IT organizations share applications as well as best-known methods.

In some industries, consortia might be non-competing companies serving the same vertical market, for example, hospital IT groups from different communities or public utilities that are assigned a monopoly over a geographical area. In other cases, open innovation consortia may include competitors. The focus is not on competitive advantage, per se, but on making the industry as a whole more efficient, perhaps by standardization paired with innovation.

Innovation budgets must remain flexible. As Curley (2004) pointed out, investments in IT are like options—their future value varies over time. Like the holder of a stock option, the innovation manager need not remain committed to a project that shows increasing signs of risk. When enterprise strategy shifts, as it often does, innovation investment managers may want to accelerate projects that are more closely related to new corporate objectives. For a company with an increased interest in reducing time-to-market, accelerating a supply-chain management innovation would better align innovative IT with corporate goals.

IT Innovation Capability

At the optimizing level of maturity, the tension between IT operational excellence and IT innovation is minimized and the groups respect each others contribution to the overall success of the enterprise. It is essential to have efficient, available, and replicated core systems, such as ERP or

Accounts Payable. Those systems should mitigate every conceivable risk. At the same time, the measured risks inherent in developing innovative IT solutions can be managed. Without innovation, the IT organization will quickly become laggards and be vulnerable to competitive pressures.

Innovation centers provide a vital role in reinventing IT and sharing new capabilities both within and beyond the company. An innovation center, which we describe in detail in Chapter 9, provides a setting for continuing education in innovative methods. The center can be a showcase for concept cars, prototypes, and fielded systems as well as a working environment for innovation in action. For companies participating in an open innovation community, the innovation center is a meeting place to share ideas with fellow travelers. Moreover, the innovation infrastructure team can complement physical centers with Web-based virtual centers as well.

The innovation creation team becomes sustaining when building better IT systems is woven into the culture of the entire enterprise. At the corporate level, innovation excellence can bolster the company's reputation. Throughout the enterprise, programs exist that reward all who sit around the innovation table—executive managers, IT innovation investment managers, infrastructure managers, and diffusion managers are all on the innovation team.

In a nutshell, the innovation capability of the IT organization is mature when information is recognized as the jet fuel for innovation across the enterprise.

Business Value Realized and Assessed

Predictability, probability, and profitability are the signals that IT innovations are delivering business value. Due to user-centered design, innovations are predictably appropriate for the IT organization's customers. At the same time, there is a high probability that innovative projects entering the pipeline will survive and reach their intended markets and deliver predicted value. This is due to excellent vetting procedures and careful pipeline management. Lastly, in an optimizing IT innovation organization, the enterprise is demonstrably more profitable due to the new ideas and improvements delivered by IT. Instrumentation is in place to actively monitor business value results.

Highly successful organizations have conquered the diffusion challenge. Marketing expertise is available in the IT organization and new IT capabilities are launched with a campaign commensurate with their scope and importance. For a modest innovation created for a limited audience, such as an improved customer tracking system for the sales department, the campaign may be no more than a workshop. For an innovation aimed at every desktop in a global company, a greater commitment to, and budget for, diffusion will be needed. The importance of *active diffusion* is now firmly cemented in place.

Through portals, workshops, and roadshows, the pipeline of IT innovations is visible throughout the organization. IT customers can see what to expect and when. As partners with IT, these customers can express satisfaction or frustration with IT capabilities and expect that IT innovators will celebrate the satisfaction and address the frustration as an opportunity.

Idea capture and management systems provide enterprise-wide support for ideas of all kinds. For example, at Intel our Innovation Engine application supports the company's technology strategic long-range planning. The systems increased the submissions of abstracts by a factor of three, and these sketches of new ideas were of higher quality. All abstracts can be viewed by everyone in the company.

Figure 4.2 provides a snapshot of the Web-enabled Innovation Engine in action. Each of the stars in the sky launches a different idea management function.

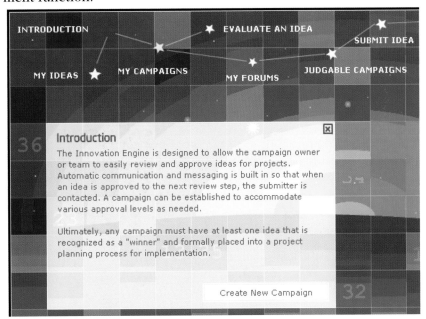

Figure 4.2 The Intel IT Innovation Engine

Source: Intel IT

The macro-process called *realize and assess the business value of IT innovations* is an autonomous process and a living reality within and beyond the IT organization.

Innovation Excellence and Operations Excellence

While daily operations of backbone systems will certainly dominate project activities in the IT organization, innovation is a recognized category of project. Several innovation projects are likely to be at different phases of their lifecycle. Using innovation infrastructure capabilities, project teams can reach customers to invite them to test versions of ideas under development. There is a growing awareness by the creation team that some aspects of innovative IT development are the same as conventional IT development and others are novel. Creating novel solutions is not an invitation to ignore software quality and careful documentation, for example.

Systemic Innovation Imperatives

For IT organizations seeking to improve their innovative capabilities, the innovation CMF provides both diagnostic and prescriptive advice, some of which we wish to underscore and highlight. Here are the major take-home messages stated as imperatives for the IT organization:

Make innovation a systemic process.   Our experience has shown us that with thought and careful management we can manage risk, chart progress, and keep innovation in alignment with corporate strategy. Innovation need not be an *ad hoc*, chaotic, and random business process.

Deliver measured business value.   While all IT systems should deliver business value, it is the innovative uses of IT that have the potential to move markets, gain competitive advantage, and dramatically improve the efficiency of business processes.

Gain and maintain management support.   We identified management support as *sine qua non* when launching an IT innovation program. It is the cornerstone to the entire CMF. And while we have described an ever-maturing innovation program, erosion of management support will quickly reverse the maturity process.

Improve maturity laterally across the macro-processes.   Generally, the IT innovation organization will be at the same maturity level across the CMF. While it is possible for the investment team to outpace the infrastructure team, the interrelationships among these four macro-processes are sufficiently robust so as to preclude advanced capability maturity in one area and basic maturity in another.

Share infrastructure with the enterprise. As we pointed out at the onset, this CMF is robust and generalizeable to other functions in the enterprise beyond IT. Our Intel *IT Innovation Engine* was developed to capture IT innovation ideas and has been generalized to capture ideas in many different functional areas of our company.

Summary

We believe that there are four key IT innovation capabilities that work together in a control loop, and we offer a capability maturity framework to identify growth in each of the four key areas. Over time and with diligence, an IT organization can improve its innovation capabilities. The IT Innovation CMF provides a roadmap. With increasing maturity, the process of innovation becomes systemic throughout the whole company, and innovation becomes a core competency and a way of life.

Chapter 5

Innovation Capability

Capability is the ability to perform actions.
In human terms capability is the sum of expertise and capacity.
—Wikipedia

Innovation capability, taken broadly, comprises the methods, tools, and skills necessary to support and streamline systemic innovation. Training courses are a part of the innovation capability, for example, because they provide the necessary skillsets for innovators. The scope of our thinking about innovation capability is as broad as our definition of systemic innovation. Workshops and courses that address ideation are within scope along with more traditional innovation capabilities such as prototyping tools and user experience design skills.

While some of the capabilities in this chapter are specific to developing and diffusing IT innovations, others are quite general and could be put to use throughout the company. Web-based idea capture and management, for example, is needed throughout the enterprise. As we shall highlight along the way, many of our Intel IT innovation capabilities are put to use outside the IT department.

We believe that Keeley's ten types of innovation and his research findings underpin the importance of disseminating innovation infrastructure throughout a company. There are opportunities to generate significant business value when innovating in the areas of finance, process, offerings, and delivery. While some innovations in the delivery of the company's products or services may require innovative IT capabilities, others may not. Systemic innovation methods can be helpful when rethinking the company's channel marketing or branding strategy, for example.

IT Innovation Project Stages

Most IT innovation process capabilities align with a stage of an innovation project. Figure 5.1 shows the stages that we use to organize our thinking.

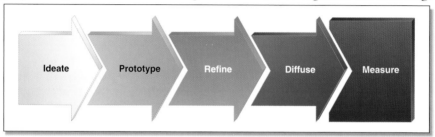

Figure 5.1 Development Stages for an Innovative IT Capability
Source: Intel IT

- Stage 1 is the ideation process—thinking of new ways to improve IT capabilities. Methods and tools for gathering information about user needs and current business processes, conceptualizing possible solutions to problems, and planning the innovation project fit in this stage.

- Stage 2 is prototyping—building inexpensive test solutions so that the feasibility of the project can be tested. Rapid prototyping tools and usability experiments are tools relevant to this stage.

- Stage 3 is refinement—extending a prototype to a full production system that is tested, integrated with other IT systems, and ready to deploy. The refinement stage also includes packaging the software, documenting its usage, and building support and training systems.

- Stage 4 is diffusion—for Intel IT, diffusing is the active acceleration of the adoption process. Since Intel IT is managed like a business, its products are actively marketed to its customers, the employees of Intel.

- Stage 5 is measurement—business value dials will be needed to translate the impact of an IT innovation into monetary terms. Without monetary units, the actual return on investment cannot be calculated. The use of business value dials is explained in Chapter 2 and Chapter 9.

Ideate

Ideation is ordinarily the first step teams use in the innovation process. Based on knowledge of a user's need obtained through observation, innovators begin by thinking about what a potential solution would look like. The outcome for the ideation stage is a solution description that is rich enough to support a prototyping effort.

Brainstorming

The ideation tool most familiar to people is the *brainstorming* process. Brainstorming is the free flow and capture of ideas in the absence of ongoing evaluation. That is, participants avoid making judgments about the ideas until the flow of ideas ends and then the ideas are evaluated. There is usually little to no structure in the brainstorming process. There are other tools and methods that rely on how the brain works or use a process to generate ideas, and brainstorming is sometimes embedded in a longer methodology. These methods are outlined below.

Brainstorming at Intel

The Intel Materials Purchasing and Management group uses an online brainstorming tool that is yielding results very quickly. When brainstorming, participants working locally and remotely participate and all ideas are captured automatically. Ideas are online and so there are no more flip charts to be transcribed nor electronic whiteboard printouts to be distributed. The tool also supports prioritization of ideas and builds an archive for future use.

Participants report the benefits to be speed, quality, and engagement. The application generates forty ideas in ten minutes and conducts a poll that enables participants to prioritize those ideas in ten more minutes. Discussion is focused and the ideas are of high quality. The team is efficient and energized by a brief but intense period of engagement.

Lateral Thinking

Lateral thinking is a method developed by Edward de Bono (1986) that helps teams examine problems from six different perspectives. It is a step-by-step process that uses techniques such as fractionation, the reversal method, and random stimulation to generate alternatives. Innovators are encouraged to identify and consider critical factors, challenge assumptions, suspend judgement, and funnel dominant ideas to final selection. The resulting ideas generated are often startling in their diversity.

To teach his method, de Bono created *six thinking hats.* By metaphorically changing hats, innovators systematically shift their perspective on the problem at hand. Most importantly, the hats help teams avoid traditional adversarial thinking and ensure that the information to make decisions about an innovation are as complete as possible.

- Blue Hat: Manager of the overall thinking process. The blue hat thinker presents the problem or opportunity and identifies where the team needs to focus and what thinking techniques ought to be employed.

- Red Hat: When donning their red hats, the team focuses on communicating feelings and intuitions. The red hat brings emotion to the forefront and helps teams to reach consensus.

- White Hat: The white hat is an invitation to share what members of the team currently knows. With all available information disclosed, the white hat thinkers identify missing information and seek it.

- Black Hat: When wearing black hats, the team takes a critical look at the solution under development. The goal is to identify risks, possible difficulties, barriers, weaknesses, or problems.

- Green Hat: The green-hat team generates ideas, captures alternatives, improves upon ideas. Putting on a green hat after wearing a black one focuses creativity at identified risks.

- Yellow Hat: With the yellow hat of optimism, the team identifies benefits, explains feasibility, and highlights the aspects of the solution that are looking good.

A facilitator leads the innovation team in looking at a problem and examining the objectives that need to be achieved. The team then tries on each *hat* in turn to extract the total picture, manage risks, identify benefits and alternatives, and reach a consensus about next steps.

At Intel, we embed ideation techniques such as lateral thinking and the Six Hats debriefing exercise into a our Systemic Innovation for Teams (SIfT) Workshop, which includes other steps in the innovation process, such as prototype development.

TRIZ

TRIZ is a methodology for solving engineering problems. Developed by Genrich Altshuller and his colleagues, the method is a collection of principles to apply one after another to generate possible solutions. Altshuller, a Russian, was a patent inspector. He based TRIZ (pronounced *trees*) on abstractions of the many clever ideas that crossed his desk.

The essence of TRIZ is the contradiction. For example, a company called OnTech came upon an interesting product packaging concept: beverages that could be stored on the shelf and could be heated at the press of a button without the aid of a stove or an oven.

The TRIZ approach suggests sharpening the contradiction and abstracting the essential feature. What's needed is a self-heating cup. The key element is heat. In the abstract, how can heat be created? Electricity, fire, and exothermic chemical reactions are three ways to produce heat.

The third approach looks promising because it is portable and exothermic reactions can be triggered by mixing chemicals. OnTech designed a three-chamber cup with chemicals in two chambers and a beverage in the third. Pressing a button breaks a seal so that the chemicals mix and the beverage is heated.

TRIZ at Intel IT

At Intel, the IT organization has a certified TRIZ trainer on our staff and we provide TRIZ workshops for the company as a whole. Those courses are ordinarily given elsewhere in the enterprise and to engineers primarily. Many of the TRIZ principles can be applied outside engineering. While we do not recommend TRIZ training for all IT professionals, TRIZ training is quite useful to software engineers and user experience designers working in the IT organization.

The heart of TRIZ is re-applied innovation. Altshuller uses previous innovations in the form of patents to spark the cognitive process that allows re-application into a new area or to solve a new problem. People that are good at pattern recognition and have a basic understanding of problem framing and engineering principles can use the TRIZ process effectively. Altshuller (1994) provides an entertaining and tractable description of TRIZ.

Ethnographic Research

Ethnographic methods are disciplined observation techniques. These methods were developed originally by anthropologists who analyzed behavior in other cultures by watching how typical human activities were undertaken. From these field notes, anthropologists extract regularities and contrast behavior in different cultures.

For IT, ethnographic methods are used to understand how people behave when performing their daily work. While not limited to the classic time-and-motion studies conducted by efficiency experts, ethnographic observations often uncover difficult tasks that slow down a process or introduce error. These challenges becomes the basis for innovative IT solutions—IT systems that fit into and assist with daily work.

Ethnographic methods are open-ended and soft. This is in contrast to focused, hard measures such as surveys and questionnaires. Often the ethnographic observation generates the hard survey item. For example, ethnography may uncover that real-time network access at meetings is helpful. A corresponding survey could then ask IT customers how often they have needed network access during a meeting.

Ethnography at Intel IT

In order to better understand Intel's enterprise needs, the IT organization conducts ethnographic research as a necessary part of the IT innovation process. A typical enthnography report would be organized as follows:

- Methodology—the purpose of the research and how will it be conducted

- Data Sets—the behavior, task, or process that is the focus of the study, the characteristics to be observed, and the data to be recorded

- User Value Statements—detailed quotes and specific observations that indicate user value along with summary statements showing what users value in general

- Implications—observed trends and relationships between users and their work environment that indicate an IT innovation opportunity

- Recommendations—conclusions drawn by the ethnographer that underscore the most important opportunities. Since ethnography is not statistical, salience must come from the observer.

In IT the ethnographers have observed both internal and external customers and the focus externally is usually in the interest of understanding how they use our IT systems to work with us efficiently. For example, Intel has migrated to a 100% eBusiness model. Intel IT assisted that effort by studying how to create better systems to handle both sides of the eBusiness interface.

A recent IT study focused on telephony choices such as wired, wireless and WiFi phones. The ethnographers studied employee phone usage throughout the workday. A key finding was that phone usage is an overall capability for employees and should not be thought of from a device perspective. That is, it's not important how the phone works, but rather how it behaves.

The ethnographers were able to extract high level requirements for any phone technology. These findings are likely to result in successful diffusion of new phone capabilities that meet users requirements. Ethnographers found that the array of options in use at Intel is inconsistent. Some phones mute, others do not, and muting commands vary. Signals such as busy were also inconsistent. Hands-free headphone capability and group-oriented speaker-phone options were irregular.

Generally, ethnography is most useful in the early days of an innovation project. We observe to understand and create requirements. We also observe the use of prototypes to see whether our solution actually meets customer requirements.

Ethnography is also useful when developing business value dials. Especially for innovations that aim to improve employee productivity, we must identify and define how our new technology improves the quality or speed with which work can be accomplished.

Prototype

Prototypes are scale models, that is, partially functional *first articles* that we use initially to test and improve upon an innovation before investing further and taking on operational risk. Prototypes share characteristics with children's toys, according to de Geus (1997). Prototypes are the systems we can afford to break in order to learn what is required for the mission-critical versions that really matter. Prototypes are also one of the most effective tools for communicating the innovation vision and obtaining buy-in from both management and users.

Concept Cars

IT concept cars are based on the same notion as automotive industry concept cars—futuristic, novel, unique, and appealing vehicles used to try out new looks and capabilities, but not necessarily fully functioning.

They have just enough definition to get across to the end users you are trying to reach (Busch 2006).

The concept car program has resulted in such prototypes as global collaboration, home monitoring, virtual team tools, an instant meeting server tool and work life effectiveness tools.

At Intel, there is an IT R&D Council that reviews requests for funding and an Innovation Assignment and Ventures program that frees people to work on the innovation.

Usage Models

A usage model is an explanation of who would use an innovation, how they would use the innovation, and what value the innovation would provide to the user and the company. Usage models are a powerful way to communicate the vision of a new application or a reapplication.

Usage Models in Action

Usage models often rest on the results of ethnographic research. When an ethnographer describes an employee struggling to perform a task, an innovator might see a way to make the task simpler. This is one way that ethnographic research is reused. A single ethnographic study could lead to the development of several usage models.

Surveys are another source of information for building usage models. In the People's Republic of China, parents reported that they have a high level of stress when they have to return to work and their child is left with a child minder. They also felt stressed when their child begins kindergarten. Kindergarten teachers claim that they are frequently interrupted by parents and grandparents that want to check on their child.

These findings led an innovator to suggest repurposing a simple remote monitoring system using web cameras and the internet. And, in fact, some kindergartens have installed cameras so that families can see their children from their personal computer.

At Intel we piloted a similar usage model. New parents could look in on their babies at home while they were at work. Off-the-shelf technologies were put to a new and innovative use. Our new parents innovated as well by inviting remote grandparents to look in on the baby as well.

User-Centered Design

User-centered design is a method of product development that is rooted in customer needs rather than in technology capabilities. IT technology companies have a history of delivering new technology capabilities and not defining how these capabilities might be used—solutions looking for problems. While both the push of technology and the pull of the customer are important, the pull of the customer is more important.

Sometimes technology push works. The somewhat-sticky glue that 3M created enabled the sticky note card that we all enjoy. More often, research and focus on the needs, wants, and limitations of the user are more effective. Business users who want to do their work efficiently and accurately will best inform the design process.

At Intel there are 4 global product design centres that are dedicated to delivering solutions that meet the unique needs of a community through user centered design. The product designs that have resulted from these centres include a PC that can be powered by a car battery during inclement weather, a mobile computing solution for children with a child-sized keyboard and a more rugged design, and an i-café PC configuration that enabled IT support teams to maintain the systems remotely.

When applied to the development of innovative IT capabilities, user centered design begins with observation—what are people currently doing and how are they equipped to do their jobs? We interview managers to understand the context of the work. And, of course, we listen to the people closest to the work. We want to know the challenges they face, the problems that they encounter, and the steps in the process that are the most error-prone or time consuming.

When we construct usage models and prototypes, we return to the user community for input. Input could be as simple as an opinion: "Does this interface make sense to you?" Input could be as precise as a study comparing elapsed time to complete a process with and without the innovative IT solution.

Sometimes the results swiftly change our direction. For example, in China, innovators wrote software to help children read and write *Hanzi* characters. The innovators used Hanzi text on the navigation menus, which worked well for adults who could read the characters. The children, however, were frustrated because they could not navigate. The product did go into production after modifications to add easier navigation.

Refine

It is traditional for IT organizations to develop their own solutions and move them into production. This approach to building innovative IT solutions is viable, to be sure, but in some cases, refinement may be better resourced outside the IT organization.

Outsource

Outsourcing can work in two ways. Some IT organizations outsource conventional IT system development so that in-house staff can focus on innovation. Who better knows the company's processes, objectives, and infrastructure? Traditionally, IT organizations aim to fully understand competitive IT capabilities and only to outsource non-strategic systems. Payroll is a common example.

Alternately, the IT organization can turn to third-parties for help in refining an innovative IT system. For projects involving new technologies, outsourcing can provide a route to scarce expertise or to skillsets not yet developed internally. In areas such as the use of RFID devices, for example, specialty consultancies can accelerate the development of new systems and reduce the risks associated with first-time deployments.

It is prudent to weigh the advantages of in-house versus out-sourced development. At Intel, we often end up constructing a hybrid form since eventually we will be deploying and supporting the new IT capabilities.

Open Source

Open source is one of the largest examples of open innovation that exists. Fuelled by people's interest in a topic and their willingness to contribute, innovative software can be developed atop components that are of high quality and available for free.

The slippery slope of open source is licensing. In most cases, the IT organization must agree to share improvements or extensions to open source components. So-called *copy-left*, in contrast to copyright, provides a legal foundation to encourage sharing. *Copy-left* is in direct conflict with intellectual property protection.

Software as a Service

Software as a service (SaaS) is an even more radical way of refining and deploying innovative IT applications. This is a delivery model where users share access to software provided by an outside vendor. The IT organization would likely qualify the vendor, but would purchase neither software nor servers. The supplier takes responsibility for whatever servers and storage systems are needed and the consumer pays a usage fee.

One distinct advantage for SaaS is access to IT expertise by small and midsize businesses. Salesforce.com and Microsoft offer sales force automation capabilities, for example, that would be difficult to support in

ProjectWish.com

A group of video game experts that routinely test new games were testing a game that was ultimately cancelled before going to final release. This group of gamers enjoyed the game so much they decided to develop their own open source game community.

The group formed an online open source community called *project wish* (www.projectwish.com) and without ever meeting each other, recently released the first deliverable, an open-source game environment called Dwarf, which won acclaim from the open-source gaming community.

Aaron Molenaur, one of the founders, gave a talk at the International Federation of Information Processing conference on Virtuality and Virtualization held in July 2007. He spoke of the overlap between gaming architecture and virtual teamwork.

ProjectWish.com developers are all over the globe. The power of open-source development is extending into all business segments and is made possible by collaboration tools in Thomas Friedman's *flat world*. (See Friedman's Flat World on page 139)

smaller businesses. Several of the early offerings available at Google Labs also demonstrate the notion of SaaS.

One might argue that paying a usage fee for a solution available to everyone is not innovative. We would reply that in the increasingly open world of IT innovation, applying SaaS to fill certain enterprise needs can be the most effective approach.

Open Innovation

In fact, more generally, IT organizations need to avoid the venerable *not invented here* syndrome and each of these different approaches to refinement highlight that need.

Diffuse

Web 2.0 Internet

Web 2.0 tools are being used to improve communications between individuals and groups. Typical Web 2.0 capabilities are as follows:

- Blogs are web logs usually maintained by an individual and are similar to a diary or journal. Bloggers record and share their activities and thoughts with others that have access to their site.

- Podcasts are audio or video recordings that can be shared among members of a community. They are another form of portable on-demand-communications.

- Social media tools include chat rooms, forums, spaces that can be personalized with profiles and photos and then shared with others. Some spaces are hidden to members at large and are only visible to those invited to participate.

College friends are staying in touch and socializing across distances by forming communities using social media tool suites. Increasingly, web-based games are being used as socialization tools as teams of people that have only met virtually get together to play cards or fight war games.

The IT Innovation Zone is an example of how we use Web 2.0. The site provides a place for Intel IT employees to share innovations, listen to

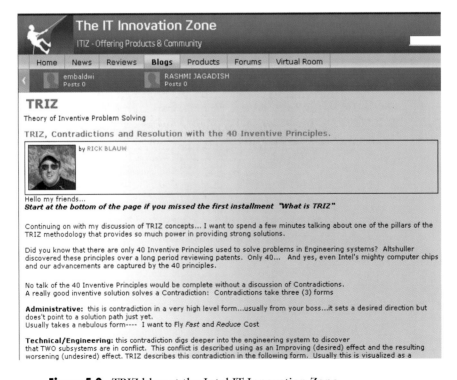

Figure 5.2 TRIZ blog at the Intel IT Innovation Zone

Source: Intel IT

podcasts, and receive support from peers. A number of Intel IT employees have blogs, such as the TRIZ blog shown in Figure 5.2.

Mashups

A mashup is the intelligent combination of XML and HTML solutions that are combined together to create a useful experience for the user. As explained in *Mashup Corporations* (Mulholland et al., 2007), the mashup enables do-it-yourself IT users to mix and match many of the Web 2.0 capabilities and tools into an environment that helps them transact their business. The term comes from the music world where disparate songs are *mashed* together to create a new song or sound.

An innovation portal that supports practitioners with many innovation products and services that can interact with each other, such as manage the pipeline, is an example of an IT innovation mashup that resulted from a service oriented architecture approach. Web services are making many mashups possible and one company using the web service of another to generate business value is going to increase in frequency. IT organizations that focus on the service experience of innovation and intelligent re-combination of services into mashups will be winners.

Crowd Sourcing

Crowd sourcing is a term coined by Wired Magazine to describe the process of taking a task ordinarily performed by an employee and offering it to a large group of people outside the organization. Google Labs provides an example of this method. Promising applications are released to early-adopter users for what was once called *alpha testing*. No promises are made that a future product will behave like the prototype. This method promotes rapid feedback. It accelerates product iteration cycles without the full overhead of completing a *beta test*.

Intel IT operates the IT Innovation Zone (ITIZ), which is quite similar to Google Labs. The IT Innovation zone at Intel is set up as a social community where users can contribute, suggest and recommend new applications which might be of use to other Intel employees. Proposed applications are vetted from a legal and security standpoint and, if they pass this test, are made available. ITIZ is rapidly evolving into an alternative IT source where some of the coolest and most useful software is made available earlier than traditionally would happen if a normal product life-cycle had been followed.

Copy-Exactly

Copy-exactly was often perceived as a barrier to innovation at Intel because every factory had to agree to an innovation before it could be adopted. Needing buy-in to an innovation from every factory raised the threshold for selection of an innovation. However, positioning the concept differently—that it would greatly improve quality— helped copy-exactly to be perceived as an innovation advantage.

Because diffusion is often the most difficult part of innovation, the guarantee of diffusion embedded in copy-exactly is a real benefit in that once an innovation is approved it is simultaneously diffused across the Intel factory network.

Other Diffusion Techniques

Workshops. Executive workshops are very effective mechanism for both diffusing innovations and building creative solutions to hard problems. A well designed workshop agenda can significantly help with the diffusion of ideas and innovations. Showcasing—whether standalone or through speakerships at conferences—is an excellent diffusion mechanisms.

Software Distribution. Automated software distribution tools can very quickly diffuse and remotely deploy applications to an entire enterprise of computers. Intel® vPro™ processor technology can remotely wake up and power on PCs, install software updates, and then shut down the systems. This kind of technology enables reliable, efficient, and fast diffusion of new innovations.

In-build. In-build is a method of distributing software and upgrades that are pushed to the client system and installed automatically as a part of the operating environment. In-build eliminates or reduces annoying upgrade messages and re-boots that are disruptive. Thus, the in-build approach helps to overcome the *interruption tolerance barrier* for adoption.

Communities of Practice. Communities of practices are a good mechanism for addressing the socialization component of innovation diffusion. The process of moving from awareness of an innovation to finding it interesting to actually using it can be enabled by socialization, and both formal and informal communities of users are effective means of diffusing innovations.

Summary

In this chapter, we have described some of the many methods and techniques available to guide IT innovators. Ideation can be stimulated with brainstorming sessions, for example, and by systematically examining emerging ideas with de Bono's lateral thinking techniques. Prototyping can take the form of a concept car, or be a first-order approximation of a system heading toward immediate development. While refinement is traditionally the work of the IT development group, we emphasized alternative ways to acquire IT capabilities, such as outsourcing or obtaining software as a service. Finally, we reviewed our thinking about how to accelerate diffusion of IT systems. We recommend leveraging the company's existing distribution channels while actively advertising the availability of new and better IT solutions.

Chapter 6

Innovation Assessment

Stairs are climbed step by step.
—Kurdish proverb

In this chapter we describe a self-assessment process that will systematically measure innovation maturity and help to chart a path to improved innovation competency. We begin by describing our self-assessment measurement instrument and explaining the steps involved in our assessment process. The assessment is designed for teams of people, which is the way projects are accomplished at Intel. We show how to use the results of the assessment to create an action plan for improvement.

The self-assessment instrument is in Appendix B. We encourage readers to peruse the instrument before reading this chapter. Our instrument was designed with Intel's core business processes in mind. We expect that other companies will develop different instruments. We offer the Intel approach as a source of ideas.

Our instrument establishes a team's level of innovation maturity. We then provide specific guidelines for moving up to the next level of the innovation capability maturity curve. Thus the instrument is integrated with our overall view that step-wise growth is a healthy approach to improving innovation capabilities.

In this chapter, we will offer suggestions about how to take advantage of this tool in both IT and non-IT organizations. We designed the instrument to apply to innovation in general—not just to IT innovation.

Intel's Innovation Self-Assessment Process

Intel's innovation self-assessment tool was designed from the beginning to be a team-based process aimed at generating a score that describes the maturity level of the group's innovation capability. In a very large group—such as an entire IT organization—a sampling of employees can be used to provide an estimate of strengths and weaknesses and a sense of the overall capability of the organization. An innovation self-assessment can also be conducted at the group or departmental level; for example, an assessment can be done within the desktop computing group.

Assessment Teams

Our focus is on teams or groups, rather than individuals or departments, because Intel uses the team as its primary way of organizing work. A typical team has a manager and five to seven members. A typical Intel employee is on two to four teams, and a line manager oversees two to four teams.

The assessment teams include diverse participants from various jobs and experience levels who are trained to discuss behavioral anchors one item at a time and to conduct consensus-based scoring to arrive at a score based on a thorough and shared understanding of the strengths and weaknesses that exist within their own organizations. From this information, the teams are able to develop specific action plans for improvements.

The actual assessment tool is reproduced in Appendix B of this book. Before reading this chapter, we suggest going to the Appendix and examining the tool itself to become familiar with the characteristics it evaluates and to review the behavioral descriptions of strengths and weaknesses in innovation capability.

The Assessment Process

During the scoring phase, the team members share their knowledge of and experience with each set of behaviors to be scored. A guideline is provided to help them come to a consensus on scores. Once the scoring phase is complete, the team members revisit their notes, consider the high and low scoring areas, and proceed to define an action plan that will address their weaknesses.

Open discussion and group interaction during the scoring phase is important because at the end of the process, the team members will need to defend their scores by providing evidence of the strengths and weaknesses identified to management to ensure management's validation and support for their action plan. Having a "group memory" of the process also reduces the risk of inconsistent scoring and promotes agreement on action plan priority tasks. Examples of action plans can be found later in this chapter.

The innovation self assessment is an annual process at Intel, with results of the assessment leading to action items that are a part of each employee's performance plan. Collectively, the action items are designed to move the team up the innovation maturity curve as successive assessments and action plans are completed.

Competencies and Behavioral Anchors

- Competencies are desirable characteristics and abilities, such as business innovation.

- Core competencies are the unique capabilities of an organization that enable it to create competitive advantage. A mature culture of innovation can be a core competency.

- Behavioral anchors are the actions, activities, and deliverables that demonstrate the achievement of a competency. They should be stated as specific, measurable, and attainable behaviors. Behavioral anchors for business innovation include observable actions such as: "Consistently proposes ideas for improvement" and "Challenges the status quo."

The Self-Assessment Framework

The innovation self-assessment tool measures six key organizational components that contribute to a culture of innovation accomplishments: management commitment, business responsibility, innovation competency, corporate values, innovation support, and innovation impact. These components and their relationships are shown in Figure 6.1. The following sections highlight the attributes or characteristics that we feel are most important to consider in a self assessment on innovation.

Figure 6.1 Components of a Self-Assessment Process
Source: Intel IT

Section 1. Management Commitment

1.1 Management Involvement
1.2 Communication of Priorities
1.3 Upward Communications
1.4 Working Innovation Policy
1.5 Innovation as a Value
1.6 Resource Allocation
1.7 Key Innovation Assets Identified

The first and fundamental step is obtaining a commitment from management to support an innovation system. In our experience, the most important section of a self-assessment tool outlines the behavioral characteristics that indicate whether management is truly involved with and committed to innovation.

Innovation as a Value

The management commitment section evaluates management's actions regarding promoting innovation and whether management appears to consider innovation important. It asks, for example, whether management communications include topics of innovation and, if so, how managers communicate about innovation delivering communication upward and how they receive and respond to communications related to innovation from upper management.

Committed managers will have a working innovation strategy or agenda. The assessment tool asks for a concrete example of a documented or communicated innovation strategy. Without evidence of such a strategy, the score will be low for this category. On the other hand, being able to show that innovation is mentioned in progress reports or written about in company publications will warrant a higher score.

Resource Allocation

The way managers allocate their resources toward innovation demonstrates management commitment more than any other behavior. The resource allocation should be well documented, and any ratios that determine the balance between innovation and other business objectives should be clearly stated. In any organization it can be difficult to obtain approval for the resources needed to develop a culture of innovation. As shown in Figure 6.2, an organization must make an initial investment in order to get the system off the ground.

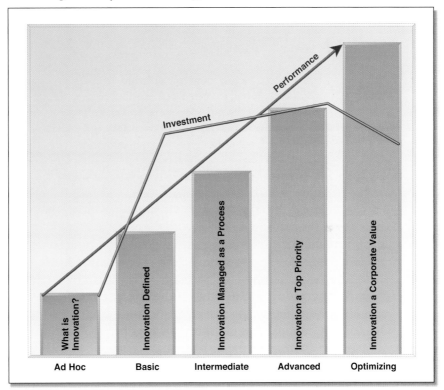

Figure 6.2 Innovation Investment Maturity Curve
Source: Intel IT

Subsequently, as the system matures, fewer resources are needed to sustain it. This is true both for the overall system and for the assessment itself. Initial users of the assessment will have to invest a quite a bit of time understanding the expectations and the areas of the instrument itself.

Key Innovation Assets Identified

Managers should also be aware of *innovation assets*—such as patent applications, intellectual property, and people with key innovation skills—and understand how their innovation funding and resources are balanced with the resources required to keep the business running as usual.

Because validation of the innovation self assessment includes defending the team's conclusions with evidence, a manager's ability to present an asset inventory to the validating senior manager can strongly support high scores.

Section 2. Business Responsibility

2.1 Organize Staff to Improve Innovation
2.2 Make Innovative Actions and Results Accountable
2.3 Adhere to Enterprise Standards for Innovation
2.4 Routinely Assess Innovative Initiatives
2.5 Involve Employees in Innovation Planning
2.6 Plan for Innovation Improvements
2.7 Discuss Innovation in Meetings and Communications

This section of the self assessment measures how the pieces of an innovation program or system work together and highlights roles and responsibilities of employees in the innovation process.

Employee roles and responsibilities should be clearly defined, and methods of measurement for accountability should be well documented. Moreover, because the use of the innovation assessment itself fits into this category, there should be a system for routine innovation assessments that includes annual and quarterly reviews of the resulting action plans. Tools and systems must be in place that enable all employees to participate, and the availability of these tools should be widely publicized.

IT employees are largely focused on keeping the business running, so it is important that their role in innovation be clearly understood and that the tools for their involvement are embedded into their routine work.

IT can also function as a catalyst for providing innovation as a service to the rest of the organization. As both users and developers of the innovation process and system, IT employees can act as subject matter experts who can facilitate and lead self-assessment sessions for other groups.

Finally, a document should exist that contains standard meeting notes and employee-management communications wherever innovation is part of the agenda.

Section 3. Innovation Competency

3.1 Innovation Training and Learning Programs
3.2 Innovation Training Improvement Process
3.3 Employee Development, and Improvement Systems

Innovation should be listed as a competency in job training plans, and an innovation curriculum that is mapped to competencies and skill development should be made available to employees.

We suggest using recognized training evaluation standards, such as Kirkpatrick's evaluation methods. Training quality and impact should be measured to ensure that they achieve their desired objectives.

Kirkpatrick's Four Levels of Learning

Donald Kirkpatrick is known for creating a four-level model for evaluating learning.

In this model, evaluation begins with level 1 (Reaction) and moves sequentially through levels 2 (Learning), 3 (Transfer), and 4 (Results). Each level is based on information from the previous level.

Level 1 evaluations simply measure how participants in a training program reacted to it—e.g., whether the information presented was useful and whether they enjoyed the sessions—because participants' reactions have important consequences for learning.

Level 2 evaluations assess the amount of learning that occurred as a result of the training program, and often use tests conducted before training to establish a baseline and again after training to determine improvements in skills, knowledge, or attitude.

Level 3 evaluations are aimed at determining whether the acquired skills, knowledge, or attitude have been subsequently incorporated into the everyday behavior of the learner.

Level 4 evaluations attempt to measure the success of the program in business value terms, such as increased production, improved quality, decreased costs, less waste, fewer accidents, increased sales, etc. While from a business perspective, such value may be the primary reason for a training program, measuring results in financial terms is difficult in itself and not easy to link directly with training. However, companies who expend the effort to develop metrics for measuring business value find it well worth the effort.

In addition, because communications play a vital role in developing, sustaining, and diffusing an innovation system, there should be a system for learning, developing, and improving communications.

Section 4. Enterprise Values

4.1 Communicate Enterprise Values
4.2 Seek Customer Input to Products and Services
4.3 Utilize Customer Input to Products and Services
4.4 Measure Customer Input to Products and Services
4.5 Include Innovation in Performance Appraisals
4.6 Track Innovation Systematically
4.7 Provide awards for innovation excellence
4.8 Apply Innovation to the Margin of the Core Business
4.9 Manage Change and Risk Systematically
4.10 Conduct Post-Project Reviews
4.11 Track Ideas, Needs, and Challenges Systematically
4.12 Adopt a Failure Management Policy
4.13 Encourage Open Participation in Innovation
4.14 Recognize and Reward Innovation Systematically
4.15 Maintain and Share Goals for Innovation

The section of the assessment that covers enterprise values measures how innovation maps to corporate values and their supporting infrastructure.

When building a culture of innovation, innovation must be clearly spelled out as a corporate value. There should be methods for both capturing and applying customer feedback on new innovations and ways of measuring innovation in products and services, such as market share, adoption rate, or even some kind of "customer excitement" index.

If innovation is an enterprise value, it should also be show up in Human Resource documents and be listed as a competency on performance appraisals. An example of including innovation competency in performance appraisals can be found in the section called Appraising Innovation Performance on page 191 of Appendix B.

Valuing innovation means not losing track of innovative ideas. As an innovation culture develops to an intermediate level of maturity, it sees the need to create an innovation pipeline so the IT organization can prioritize and track projects through prototyping, development, and deployment.

As the organization proceeds up the innovation maturity curve, it will encourage innovation by establishing a reward and recognition system for various forms of innovation—tangible and intangible, financial and non-financial. All employees should be encouraged to participate in fostering innovation, and awards for innovation excellence should range from low-level peer-to-peer recognition up to corporate-level and industry-level awards.

Finally, there should also be a reward system for benefiting from mistakes and learning lessons from conducting post-mortem reviews of projects that were not successful.

Mapping Innovation to Corporate Values

At Intel, an exercise to explicitly map innovation to our corporate values resulted in the following statements. Other IT organizations can perform the same exercise by printing a copy of their corporate values and discussing how each one of them relates to innovation. Questions to ask include "How does this value benefit from innovation?" and "How does it contribute to innovation?"

Customer orientation: We listen to our customers or stakeholders and respond to their needs in innovation, as research shows that most innovations can be tracked to customer input.

Discipline: An annual performance appraisal includes innovation as an item by which performance is measured. This supports risk taking and other Intel values and accelerates innovation through disciplined measurement systems.

Quality: We foster innovation in our work, products, and services. Much of our innovation involves incremental improvement to existing products and services to maintain high quality.

Risk taking: Innovation occurs when we challenge the status quo and embrace change. Innovation thrives on success and benefits from mistakes. Informed risk taking is rewarded. To assess risk taking and innovation, we hold meetings after projects are complete to learn from our successes and failures.

Great place to work: A challenging work environment provides our diverse employees with an opportunity to innovate; they are rewarded and recognized for their innovation.

Results orientation: We set challenging and competitive goals such as staying one generation ahead of the competition and reducing our TCO, and innovation helps us achieve those goals.

Section 5. Innovation Support

5.1 Processes for Innovation
5.2 Use of Innovation Experts
5.3 Use of IT Systems to Support Innovation
5.4 Business Planning and Innovation

The Innovation Support section of the assessment measures the role of innovation experts and enterprise infrastructure and tools—such as intranet websites, Internet websites, online support systems, virtual innovation centers, and online training and education—in supporting innovation.

When we think of innovation experts, we think of Gladwell's descriptions of the different roles certain individuals can play to support the diffusion of new ideas. He describes some people as *connectors*—individuals with very large social circles who can deliver strong endorsements for new ideas to a large group of people. Guiding the connectors are *mavens*—people who are extremely knowledgeable about certain aspects of a market or a technology. (See Gladwell's Tipping Point on page 138) At Intel we also rely on subject matter experts, on pathfinders who are willing venture into uncharted territory, on champions who can effectively promote and support ideas, and on sponsors who can help us find funding for them.

Section 6. Impact of Innovation

6.1 Inventory of Innovations
6.2 Business Value of Innovations

The last section of the self assessment measures the impact of innovation accomplishments and details innovation performance results. It also provides a way for employees to measure how innovative the company's products and services are.

As we stated at the beginning of this section, management commitment is the foundation for combining business responsibility, innovation competency, corporate values, and innovation support to ultimately produce innovation impact.

Evidence that the self-assessment process has resulted in innovation capability maturity can clearly be seen in a well-designed and managed innovation pipeline and in the development and routine use of metrics that clearly show the business value of innovations that come out of it.

Scoring the Self Assessment

We recommend beginning the scoring process by asking our teams to examine each scoring category as a basis for determining how their particular environment measures up with the examples of an optimized innovation environment listed in the right-hand column of the self assessment tool shown in Appendix B. To accomplish this, the teams share their observations and experiences and write statements that describe the current state of their group's innovation capability.

For example, in Self-Assessment Section 1.1, Management Involvement, the standard for an optimized innovation environment would be one in which:

- An innovation strategy has been defined.
- The manager discusses and values innovation.
- Innovation assessment is conducted annually.
- Team innovation is recognized and rewarded.

The team members come up with a list of descriptions of their own group's progress with respect to these standards and then come to a consensus about the overall maturity of their system using the scoring chart shown in Table 6.2 as a reference for allocating points within each category.

For example, a team's statements about management involvement in a group might include the following list:

- An innovation strategy has not been defined.
- Our manager often discusses and seems to value innovation.
- An innovation assessment is conducted annually.
- Team innovation is rarely recognized and rewarded.

Table 6.3 can be used as a guideline for scoring. For example, the team members might generally agree that they are in the beginning (10-30%) level and, after discussion, come to a consensus to give that category a score of 25 out of 50.

Table 6.1   Assessment Scoring Summary

Management Commitment	Points Possible
1.1 Management Involvement	50
1.2 Communication of Priorities	50
1.3 Upward Communications	20
1.4 Working Innovation Policy	30
1.5 Innovation as a Value	30
1.6 Resource Allocation	30
1.7 Key Innovation Assets Identified	30
Business Responsibility	
2.1 Organize Staff to Improve Innovation	50
2.2 Make Innovative Actions and Results Accountable	50
2.3 Adhere to Enterprise Standards for Innovation	50
2.4 Routinely Assess Innovative Initiatives	30
2.5 Involve Employees in Innovation Planning	30
2.6 Plan for IT Innovation Improvements	30
2.7 Discuss Innovation in Meetings and Communications	20
Innovation Competency	
3.1 Innovation Training and Learning Programs	40
3.2 Innovation Training Improvement Process	20
3.3 Employee Development, and Improvement Systems	10
Enterprise Values	
4.1 Communicate Enterprise Values	20
4.2 Seek Customer Input to Products and Services	20
4.3 Utilize Customer Input to Products and Services	20
4.4 Measure Customer Input to Products and Services	20
4.5 Include Innovation in Performance Appraisals	20
4.6 Track Innovation Systematically	20
4.7 Provide awards for innovation excellence	10
4.8 Apply Innovation to the Margin of the Core Business	10
4.9 Manage Change and Risk Systematically	10
4.10 Conduct Post-Project Reviews	10
4.11 Track Ideas, Needs, and Challenges Systematically	20
4.12 Adopt a Failure Management Policy	20
4.13 Encourage Open Participation in Innovation	20
4.14 Recognize and Reward Innovation Systematically	20
4.15 Maintain and Share Goals for Innovation	10
Innovation Support	
5.1 Processes for Innovation	70
5.2 Use of Innovation Experts	30
5.3 Use of IT Systems to Support Innovation	20
5.4 Business Planning and Innovation	20
Impact of Innovation	
6.1 Inventory of Innovations	120
6.2 Business Value of Innovations	120
Total Points	**1200**

We offer the following guidelines for determining a maturity score.

Table 6.2   Rating an Innovation System's Maturity.

Maturity score	Maturity Level
100%	World class system: ■ Comprehensive documentation ■ Catalyst for other organizations ■ Vision plus organization and management commitment ■ Permanent innovation ■ Innovation culture
70% - 90%	Excellent system: ■ Consistently good documentation ■ Frequent innovation ■ Established innovative culture
40% - 60%	Good system: ■ Generally good documentation ■ Good results in several areas ■ Committed management support ■ Frequent innovation
10% - 30%	Beginning of system: ■ Limited documentation ■ Occasional innovation
0%	No system: ■ No documentation available ■ Lack of innovation ■ No innovation vision or organizational support

Source: Intel IT

Developing an Action Plan

Having completed the scoring of the self assessment, the team proceeds to create an action plan that will be presented to their senior managers for approval. During this stage, the team looks at the lowest scores and areas of highest concern in relationship to the value dials that the organization wants to manage.

They capture three types of information in each category to use in developing the action plan:

- Highlights—areas where evidence is strong about their innovation capabilities.

- Lowlights—places where the discussion revealed weaknesses, lack of evidence, or problems with the innovation system.

- Action items—actions that the team itself can initiate to catalyze improvement in their group. We have found that it is important to prioritize the actions and commit to what reasonably can be done in order to build confidence in future success.

- Recommendations—suggestions for actions management could take to facilitate innovation. For example, for a lowlight stated as "People are not recognized for innovation, and they don't know the expectations for innovation performance," a recommendation could be that HR and management should include innovation as an item in performance appraisals and include behavioral anchors to clarify expectations.

Figure 6.3 and Figure 6.4 show examples of two quarterly action plans developed by the same group, six months apart. The initial action plan illustrates how teams set basic goals and objectives for gaining innovation competence. The subsequent action plan shows that competency is improving and that new and higher expectations are set.

Figure 6.3 Initial Action Plan

ACTION PLAN: Q4 07	
Evidence of a System Highlights	**Areas of Potential Improvements (Lowlights)**
• We maintain a website telling customers what's new and next from our organization. • Post project reviews are part of our methodology.	Low scores on management involvement: • Innovation is rarely mentioned in status meetings. • Innovation is not listed as a competency in job training. • People are not recognized for innovation, and they don't know the expectations for their performance as innovators. Low scores for utilizing customer input to products and services: • Customer satisfaction scores are dropping. • We don't feed complaints into the innovation process. • Many customers are unaware of our interest in input. • We focus our customers on services more than products. • We have no regular, predictable recognition process.

Actions to take

• Include innovation as a regular agenda item for our weekly staff meetings.

• Include innovation activities in progress reports.

• Find an innovation champion for our group.

• Contribute more frequently to the corporate newsletter.

• Include mention of innovation in job training.

• Revisit previous post-project reviews before launching new projects.

• Give recognition to the developers of the What's New website and the operations manager at the next department-wide meeting.

• Monitor the use of help systems to assess customer needs. Work with management to install a recognition system into existing systems. .

Recommendations

• Include innovation goals in department plans.

• Develop a clear mission statement that includes innovation.

• HR and management should include innovation as performance appraisals and provide employees with the performance behavioral anchors that they can use to measure it.

• Hold quarterly contests to seek out new ideas from customers.

• Communicate that innovation is equal to other business priorities.

Source: Intel IT

Figure 6.4 Subsequent Action Plan

ACTION PLAN: Q2 08	
Evidence of System Highlights	**Areas of Potential Improvements (Lowlights)**
• Innovation is on the regular staff agenda and is discussed at most of our meetings.	• There is no explicit innovation training curriculum, training sessions are merely motivational.
• Innovation articles have become part of corporate publications.	• It is difficult to find time or funds for innovative projects.
• We have improved our What's New website.	• We have no budget for innovation.
• Innovation is now listed as a competency in job training.	• Low scores on processes for innovation:
• Our appraisal process explicitly identifies innovation as a competency and includes behavioral anchors for innovation.	• We collect ideas, but rarely take action to use them.
• We have an annual award for the best innovation.	• Our ideas are stored in email messages.
• Individuals can nominate others for recognition.	

Actions to take
• Provide feedback on training courses so instructors can improve them.
• Give recognition for all major highlights in this assessment.
• Present data to senior management on market share competitors' innovation programs and processes and communicate a sense of urgency.

Recommendations
• Provide a physical innovation environment.
• Have innovation experts work with training department to develop innovation training curriculum.
• Make a course on ethnography available.
• Create a website for capturing and tracking customer ideas.
• Establish online tools for sharing ideas and requirements throughout the organization.

Source: Intel IT

Moving to the Next Maturity Level

This section provides examples of how an organization can use action plans as a springboard to proactively advance to the next capability level within a category.

In order to cover a cross-section of the Self Assessment Tool, we have selected one category in each of the Self-Assessment Tool's six sections—Management Commitment, Business Responsibility, Innovation Competency, Enterprise Values, Innovation Support, and Impact—to use as an example of how to steadily move through the maturity stages from Level 1 (Initial) to Level 5 (Optimizing).

We have chosen the following sections:

- Section 1.1—Management Involvement
- Section 2.1—Organize Staff to Improve Innovation
- Section 3.1—Innovation Training and Learning Programs
- Section 4.7—Provide Awards for Innovation Excellence
- Section 5.3—Use of IT Systems to Support Innovation
- Section 6.2—Business Value of Innovations

Management Commitment

Management Involvement (Section 1.1)

Level 1: Initial

At the initial level, management is primarily concerned with efficiency and cost-effectiveness and tends to view innovation as a financial risk. There is no budget for creative opportunities and no infrastructure to support them. Senior management is not involved in innovation processes, and if innovation occurs at all, it happens by accident.

Steps to take to attain Level 2:

- Present data to senior management on market-share competitors' innovation programs and processes.
- Present self-assessment and benchmark data to senior management.
- Introduce innovation programs to address known problems—e.g., IT Efficiency items that require improvement—and top Pareto items—i.e., the 20% of activities that produce 80% of the benefits.

Level 2: Beginning

At this level, senior management is beginning to be aware of value of innovation, but—while no longer averse to discussions of it—they are not yet enthusiastic. At this stage an innovative project is usually driven by a hero.

While there is no budget for innovative projects, management can be persuaded into freeing up resources for a pet project. Funding at this level is based upon whether management likes the idea instead of on hard data. Most of the innovation that actually occurs is related to product development.

Senior management has come to realize that not innovating can be costly, and they are aware of competitive threats, but they are still likely to see spending on innovation as jeopardizing their R&D budgets.

Steps to take to attain Level 3:

■ Present innovation indicators and data per individual organization or department to senior management.

■ Actively work with management to identify innovative solutions to issues.

Level 3: Intermediate

Senior management understands the competitive advantage of being seen as an innovative company, and some even see it as a competitive necessity. Moreover, as management sees efficiency gains and cost reductions resulting from IT innovations, the innovation budget is poised to grow. At this level, senior management is on the verge of deciding that innovative excellence is a core competency. While innovation has not yet been incorporated into business operations, management is providing oversight and visibility and is beginning to hold business units accountable for innovation performance.

Innovation is now beginning to become part of the company's culture and is now supported by a formal budget.

Metrics for determining the business value of innovations are being developed, as are standard methods for managing innovation. Most projects at this stage have an innovation component.

Steps to take to attain Level 4:

■ Present business value data to senior management.

■ Obtain senior management's commitment to take a more active role in ensuring an innovative place to work.

■ Define an innovation strategy.

Level 4: Advanced

At this level, emphasis has shifted from creating business value to maximizing it, and managers are now paying increased attention to longer term planning. Investment managers have formalized business value measures.

A clearly defined innovation strategy is in place with explicit goals and priorities. The innovation pipeline management process has become more refined and the queue of projects is managed with strong skillsets, purposeful diffusion, and supporting IT capabilities.

Innovation is becoming incorporated into business operations and is managed in the same way that quality, safety, yield, etc., are managed.

As there are more innovation ideas in the pipeline than can be handled, the ideas must be prioritized, and a business case is required for new innovation opportunities.

Innovation experts are highly respected and viewed as partners, and the culture of innovation has enhanced the organization's reputation in the eyes of its customers and trading partners.

Steps to take to attain Level 5:

- Present information around value- and results-based innovation programs.
- Facilitate senior management through this educational process.
- Work to define what the next level is for the organization.

Level 5: Optimizing

At this level of maturity, business value is routinely measured and realized.

Innovation is seamlessly integrated into business operations, and the innovation pipeline is visible throughout the organization by means of web portals, workshops, and road shows. A system for active diffusion of innovation is in place.

Business Responsibility

Organize Staff to Improve Innovation (Section 2.1)

Level 1: Initial

There is an innovation expert or designated individual within the company who champions innovation.

Steps to take to attain Level 2:

- Begin to establish awareness for improving innovation.
- Develop company innovation expectations for higher-use work environments, such as R&D, Product Design Centers, and problem solving teams.
- Make experts available for coaching and consulting.

Level 2: Beginning

Innovation is site-specific. However, an innovation team or committee has been formed, and innovation has champions.

Steps to take to attain Level 3:

- Establish innovation expectations with the innovation team or committee members.
- Communicate and sell innovation expectations via the innovation committee members.
- Establish the "norming" innovation behaviors.

Level 3: Intermediate

Site innovation experts are role models for innovation, but management and supervisors are also starting to become role models for innovative behaviors. Employees participate in efforts to drive changes.

Steps to take to attain Level 4:

- Management formally communicates their endorsement of role modeling innovation through staff meetings, etc.
- Innovation experts help to identify more industry innovation concepts and practices for the organization, e.g., benchmarks, best-known methods, etc.

Level 4: Advanced

By this point all of management is aware of innovation as a business process and routinely demonstrates commitment. Innovation experts help organizations to focus on training and behaviors.

Steps to take to attain Level 5:

■ Establish training, and work with the customer group to develop an approach to remove barriers to innovation.

■ Develop indicators to track the group's performance.

■ Encourage management to establish innovation as a core value.

■ Expand the organization's behavioral focus on innovation to the industry environment.

Level 5: Optimized

All employees in the organization are committed to innovation and focus on behaviors that foster it.

Innovation Competency

Innovation Training and Learning Programs (Section 3.1)

Level 1: Initial

At this level, either no training exists or training in innovation is very informal. If there is informal training, it is merely the result of *ad hoc* support and interest.

Steps to take to attain Level 2:

■ Identify core innovation training requirements.

■ Look for packaged innovation training programs to leverage innovation resources.

Level 2: Beginning

Basic innovation training is available and was probably developed to ensure consistency and terminology. Training sessions are typically led by innovation staff and committee members.

Steps to take to attain Level 3:

■ Have innovation experts begin to work with peers to establish a formal training program based upon competencies, policies, and known gaps.

■ Have innovation experts solicit volunteers to teach the classes.

Level 3: Intermediate

The innovation curriculum has been expanded, and instructors are now from the innovation core group or interested volunteers. Web-based systems are available to support innovation training.

At this level, training assessment processes are formalized and data — including baseline data—is collected.

Steps to take to attain Level 4:

■ Have innovation experts engage the customers in the training process (e.g., creating, revising, etc.).

■ Have innovation experts and the customers begin to establish certification packages based upon job criteria.

■ Have innovation experts partner with business management to provide resources for teaching innovation courses.

Level 4: Advanced

Online tools from Human Resources and job competency diagrams include innovation concepts. Business units are responsible for tracking of training. Training classes are routinely being reviewed for quality.

Steps to take to attain and maintain Level 5:

■ Establish behavior-based training.

■ Have business groups take over tracking and integration of innovation training in their everyday business.

■ Provide site-specific information from business units to training.

■ Identify additional courses to meet future innovation needs.

■ Ensure that training programs are aligned with policy and philosophy of the organization.

■ Base revisions to training courses on feedback from all major stakeholders.

Level 5: Optimized

Business groups own training and ensure quality. The business organization ensures that resources are available to teach classes. Innovation training is integrated with all other operationally required training courses.

Enterprise Values

Provide Awards for Innovation Excellence (Section 4.7)

Level 1: Initial

Management has been provided information on basics and benefits of an innovation. Innovation awareness is promoted through posters and other symbols.

Innovation committees are not process-oriented, and reactions to innovation tend to be based on personal perception rather than on business value data or analysis.

Steps to take to attain Level 2:

■ Establish an innovation committee/team/interest group meeting process and develop an education package for the members.

■ Have innovation experts work with innovation committees to establish a recognition system based on innovation suggestions.

■ Establish visible identity of innovation committee members in the work place.

Level 2: Beginning

Basic systems are in place for establishing an innovation committee, an innovation suggestions pipeline, and chasm crossing. Awareness is increased by innovation poster contests and innovation campaigns.

Steps to take to attain Level 3:

■ Innovation experts work with management to implement a more advanced recognition system.

■ Use self-assessments and action plans to improve innovation performance.

■ The innovation committee works with HR and management to implement innovation as a line item in focal review.

Level 3: Intermediate

The organization has developed a system to recognize employees for innovations, suggestions, and ideas. Innovation rewards have been established for employee performance. The innovation staff is expected to solve problems, and the focus is on engineering solutions.

Steps to take to attain Level 4:

- Have innovation experts work with management to further integrate a recognition system into the organization's culture.

- Incorporate innovation training into all other operationally required training courses.

- Establish expanded innovation expectations in the focal review process.

Level 4: Advanced

An innovation recognition system is incorporated into the organization's business recognition system, and innovation expectations are incorporated into the annual review process.

Steps to take to attain and maintain Level 5:

- Increase visibility of recognition and awards for innovation through the normal business recognition systems, such as large staff meetings, website publication, and Intel Achievement Awards.

Level 5: Optimizing

The innovation recognition system is self-sustaining and inherent to success.

Innovation Support

Use of IT Systems to Support Innovation (Section 5.3)

Level 1: Initial

Innovation is handled by Intel Legal and Human Resources for the purpose of protecting intellectual property. There is no established process for harvesting and capturing ideas. Locally developed tools exist, but with low adoption levels and manual processes.

Steps to take to attain Level 2:

- Get innovation experts involved in driving innovation awareness.

Level 2: Beginning

Innovation experts support innovation campaigns by recruiting subject matter experts to perform vetting of all innovation campaign ideas and inputs. Interest is increasing for providing a physical innovation environment.

Steps to take to attain Level 3:

- Have innovation experts encourage innovation committees to use industry tools, processes, value metrics, and standards to manage the pipeline.

Level 3: Intermediate

At this level, senior management realizes that commitment and participation is required for an innovation infrastructure and innovation systems.

The Innovation Committee reviews innovation ideas and is involved in the pipeline management process. Campaigns are conducted by site or group innovation staff.

Innovation indicators and pipeline evaluation reports begin to be created by business operations in partnership with innovation experts. Engineering or technical solutions are expected to complete the pipeline management process.

Steps to take to attain Level 4:

- Have innovation experts work with management to develop innovation review meetings and steering committees.
- Assess the quality of tools and processes to evaluate the system.
- Use data to emphasize behavior as a leading indicator of innovation.

Level 4: Advanced

Business units drive innovation review meetings, and management representatives from all key areas are being reviewed. Innovation experts are engaged in the process.

Business owners perform all pipeline management processing using a standard suite of tools.

The focus is now on employee innovation skills, training, and behaviors. Innovation ideas, problems, and challenges are starting to be seen as assets to be managed to their best end value.

Steps to take to attain and maintain Level 5:

- Have innovation experts ensure that management understands the need to include innovation in their management meetings.

- Have innovation experts work with management to move them from using lagging indicators to leading indicators.

Level 5: Optimizing

An innovation pipeline review is incorporated into the same level of operations as reviews of quality and business value.

Business owners routinely assess all pipeline gates to manage innovations to their best end value.

Innovation experts process and support all innovation campaign outputs, tools, and processes, but now only need to advise business owners on complex items.

Impact of IT Innovation

Business Value of Innovations (Section 6.2)

Level 1: Initial

Management is focused on stock prices and market share as indicators of business value. Innovation goals are established by senior management and are typically focused on the number of patents, number of invention disclosure forms, etc.

Steps to take to attain Level 2:

- Obtain innovation cost data from finance.
- Define the need for a tracking system.
- Review innovation investment data to establish a baseline for costs and funding.
- Initiate a business value reporting philosophy.
- Establish a forum to report business value goals to management.
- Create a tracking system for innovation information and begin tracking indicators.

Level 2: Beginning

Metrics have expanded to include business value and innovation index items. Senior management or innovation committee members have established innovation goals that are included in business operation goals.

Steps to take to attain Level 3:

- Track lagging indicators for management to use in business plans.
- Establish broader goals to improve innovation indicators.

Level 3: Intermediate

Metrics are focused on lagging indicators. Management is including innovation goals in business planning, and linking them with other corporation goals.

Management is beginning to associate goals for innovation business value and ROI with their level of innovation investment.

Steps to take to attain Level 4:

- Utilize self-sustaining tracking and reporting mechanisms for pipeline management and engine reports.
- Have innovation experts work with the business organization to develop new metrics for measuring their performance.

Level 4: Advanced

The organization has world-class innovation rates and metrics and is looking for new metrics to drive innovation improvements. Unique innovation business goals have been established along with other business goals to drive improvements within their operations.

Steps to take to attain and maintain Level 5:

- Define and use leading indicators to help measure group performance, such as "number of innovation communications."
- Develop innovation surveys and other ongoing feedback systems to assess performance.
- Continue to look for new indicators to drive improvements in areas of identified need.

Level 5: Optimizing

At this level, business value is forecast, measured, and reported.

Senior management has come to rely on leading indicators, employee surveys, and formal assessment of management systems.

Business groups are responsible for establishing innovation goals, based on employee surveys, feedback, and leading indicators.

The Importance of Innovation Assessment

Innovation assessment is an important tool for establishing a baseline measurement of an organization's level of maturity in innovation. It enables a team, group, or organization to develop explicit plans to increase maturity over time. It also serves as a *de facto* training tool for both the employees who perform the assessment and the managers who review them.

At Intel, when several teams have completed the assessment, senior management compare scores and profiles across the larger organization. Table 6.3 shows assessment results for four teams.

■ While teams A and B have identical total scores, their profiles are quite different and revealing. Team B has superior innovation capabilities, but they have not been able to contribute to innovation in the company's products and services. While Team A needs additional training across the board, Team B needs some management attention to align their work with the offerings of the company.

■ Team C is at an intermediate level of competence and should be encouraged to continue acquiring and polishing innovation skills and methods.

■ Team D is in trouble, and the problem probably starts with a lack of management commitment. If management commitment is lacking, then all remaining assessment categories have low scores.

Profiles like those shown in Table 6.3 provide feedback to supervisors, first line managers, and team leaders. The very process of measuring and comparing scores often increases management commitment.

Table 6.3   Cross-organizational Comparison of Completed Assessments

	Team A	Team B	Team C	Team D
1. Management Commitment	49%	92%	75%	16%
2. Business Responsibility	40%	85%	64%	12%
3. Innovation Competence	41%	97%	56%	7%
4. Intel Values	40%	84%	70%	32%
5. Innovation Support	45%	46%	91%	24%
6. Impact	42%	46%	60%	10%
7. Products and Services	42%	5%	80%	0%
Total	43%	43%	75%	9%

Source: Intel IT

Summary

Assessment is sometimes viewed as a threatening process, but we believe it can be at the heart of a learning process. A thorough appraisal of a team's innovation capabilities provides a foundation for growth. Our five-level capability maturity framework identifies a developmental path. Management commitment and measured objectives in the team's action plans together ensure that innovation skills will improve over time.

Chapter 7

Innovation Pipeline Management

Prediction is very difficult, especially about the future.
—Niels Bohr

As advances in information technologies fuel creativity, vision, and prototyping, companies will find that they have a backlog of innovation ideas that is larger than the IT innovation budget can support. In addition, innovative IT projects often present a greater management risk since they often depend on new technology ingredients. And, the IT organization's overall project pipeline contains a mix of innovative IT projects along with well-proven systems necessary for the daily operations of the company.

One solution is to bypass the IT pipeline and manage innovative IT projects separately. While this is an understandable alternative, it does amplify several risks. For example, sidestepping disciplined software development methods raises the risk of creating production systems that are unstable. Also, proper integration of innovative systems with the IT infrastructure, and other IT systems is less likely if innovative IT solutions are developed outside of the mainstream process.

We believe that innovative IT projects should be managed along with other IT projects, but with a different management framework. For example, it may make sense to actively accelerate or retard the progress of an innovative IT project, whereas this is rarely acceptable for conventional IT projects.

The IT Innovation Pipeline

The goal of pipeline management for innovative IT projects is to determine the value potential and relevance of the projects and expedite productization of those with the most value, both within and outside of the enterprise. The traditional value path leads from research to operations within the company. Alternately, some innovations exit the company to be developed by others. And, some innovations are purchased from others and released into the pipeline late in the process.

The innovation pipeline management process is aimed at keeping a close watch on the innovation pipeline, cultivating the options it contains, and steering candidate innovation projects toward the most appropriate value path. Intel IT's innovation pipeline management methodology identifies five stages and the three basic product life cycles value paths shown in Figure 7.1.

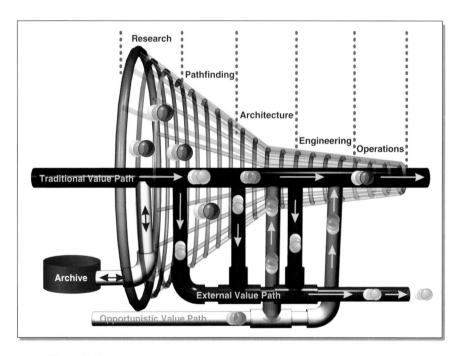

Figure 7.1 Pipeline Stages and Value Paths for Innovative IT Products and Services

Source: Intel IT

Pipeline Stages

Note that there are multiple entry and exit points to the pipeline stages, which we shall describe below. Stages in the innovation pipeline are as follows:

- *Research*: At this stage, researchers are establishing a scientific foundation of information which is not yet aimed at solving real-world problems. Universities and government research laboratories are good partners at this stage. The development of the mouse at Stanford Research Institute and the invention of object-oriented programming at Xerox PARC are examples of research findings.

- *Pathfinding and Technology Development*: The pathfinding stage comprises early efforts to marry newly-discovered facts and relationships to build platforms and solutions. Some IT organizations have individuals or teams that perform this role, especially those with researchers.

  Early adopters often have the skills that lend themselves to be pathfinders as part of their natural propensity to seek out the new and novel. Those that are good at recognizing patterns and emerging trends also make good pathfinders.

  For IT, corporate research groups and start-up companies can play the role of pathfinding. The Xerox Alto, the first computer designed for use by an individual, is an example of a pathfinder's result.

- *Architecture*: At the architecture stage, the platforms and solutions provided by pathfinders are organized into functional systems. Architectures emerge as IT suppliers compete to establish standard interfaces among component technologies. The client-server architecture is an example of an architecture that emerged as networks merged personal computers and shared computing resources.

- *Engineering*: Guided by an architecture, IT organizations assemble and test solutions that address the information processing needs of the enterprise. Common problems give rise to suppliers who exploit economies of scale to engineer and sell standard solutions. Enterprise resource planning (ERP) and customer relationship management (CRM) are two examples of pre-engineered solutions available to IT organizations.

■ *Operations*: Whether custom built or based on packaged software, IT solutions exit the engineering stage and are put into operations. At this stage, IT operations focus on making solutions efficient and available while IT diffusion managers aim to bring solutions into usage as quickly as possible so that business value will begin to accrue.

Organizations vary in their appetite for participating in the early stages of IT innovation. Generally, larger and more information-dependent enterprises participate earlier in the pipeline. Global financial services firms, for example, were early participants in hammering out secure networks that could be trusted to carry currency transactions (e.g., SWIFT). Similarly, supply-line management systems were engineered by consortia building systems for the automotive and electronic industries.

Midsize and smaller companies most commonly innovate by purchasing packaged software and tailoring it to their needs. While two decades ago, the build vs. buy decision often led to a coding effort in COBOL, in recent years the quality and variety of pre-engineered solutions have dominated the IT solution set. As described by Rogers (2003) and Moore (1991), these companies are generally a part of the early and late majority. Their use of innovative IT solutions is signaled when successful products cross Moore's chasm.

Pipeline Value Paths

As Figure 7.1 on page 114 also illustrates, innovation projects have three distinct value paths, as follows:

■ *Traditional value path:* On the conventional path, IT projects move results from research activities and transform them into production systems ready for deployment. As noted, this path is typical on the IT supply side, but increasingly rare on the IT demand side.

■ *Opportunistic value path:* Especially for innovative IT projects that adapt and reapply technology previously developed for other usage, it is possible to bring a project into the pipeline relatively late. This is accomplished by licensing technology from third-party vendors. The opportunistic path is also used when IT organizations redeploy existing technology solutions and adapt them to other company needs.

■ *External value path:* IT research organizations occasionally produce inventions that, while valuable, are not consistent with the strategy of the enterprise. These innovations have the potential to become products. Innovation on this value path move out of the pipeline and are licensed to third-parties for productization and diffusion.

Our value paths are similar in many ways to Chesbrough's open innovation model. The multiple paths reflect the fact that innovative IT projects are qualitatively different than ordinary IT. Upgrading storage capacity, fielding a new database in support of compliance requirements, and extending network infrastructure are the types of traditional activities that IT must deliver on time and on budget. Projects such as Intel's ergonomic advising software or Miramar, on the other hand, may follow different paths within and outside Intel.

Most IT innovations return financial value in dollar terms, while some return value in less tangible benefits, such as increased employee safety, improved IT customer satisfaction, or enhancement of the firm's reputation. Using an options management tool like a business value index can help manage and assess the value potential of putative innovations.

Miramar

Miramar is an example of the commercialization path to value. Intel IT Innovation and Research developed an advanced 3-D collaboration prototype we called *Miramar*. After a business case analysis, the IT organization decided that it should not fund the full development. Instead, we licensed the prototype and its underlying technologies to an external company, QWAQ, who branded their product *QWAQ Forum*. In return for our technology, QWAQ will provide Intel with a full license to use the *QWAQ Forum* product and we will receive royalties from QWAQ sales as well.

Managing the IT Innovation Pipeline

There are decisions to be made when formulating a management strategy for an IT innovation pipeline. In this section, we shall outline the available choices, the key decisions that need to be made, and the route that we have taken at Intel IT. Our roadmap, shown in Figure 7.2, takes a clean-sheet approach, that is, the roadmap creates a management approach from scratch. There are six basic steps.

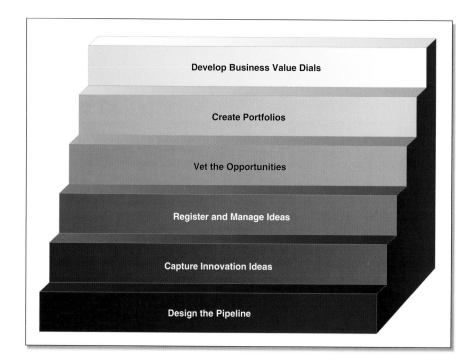

Figure 7.2 Formulating an IT Innovation Pipeline Management Strategy
Source: Intel IT

Step 1: Design the Pipeline

There are three key decisions to be made about the pipeline design: will it follow an open innovation model or a closed, proprietary model, will innovative projects be mixed with conventional IT projects or will the types be managed separately, and will innovation be a centralized IT function or a function distributed throughout the organization? The decisions can be made independently, as shown in Figure 7.3.

Advantages and Disadvantages of Different Models

Distributed versus Centralized Innovation. The founders of Intel felt strongly that innovation should be distributed throughout the company's operations. In their prior experience, Robert Noyce, Gordon Moore and Andy Grove realized that centralized innovation often generated ideas that never left the research laboratory. A tradition was established, not to centralize innovation, which carries through today. Intel IT innovation is pervasive and distributed, both within the IT organization and across the corporation as a whole.

Centralization of innovation may be a more effective model for companies who create IT products, that is, for the supply side of IT. And, centralization may help the longer-term innovative process and increase the likelihood of a radical breakthrough. As noted, centralized research facilities such as SRI International and Xerox PARC did provide radical

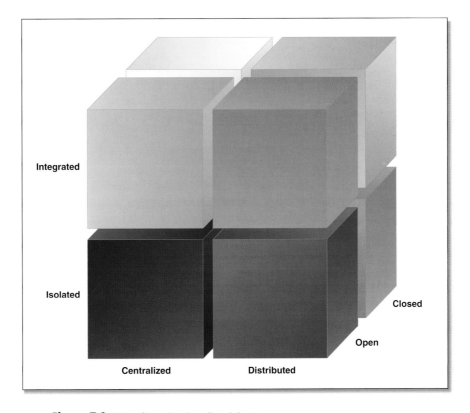

Figure 7.3 Pipeline Design Decisions

Source: Intel IT

innovations, although it is useful to point out that both institutions failed to deliver business value.

Integrated versus Isolated Pipelines.   At Intel, we integrate innovative IT projects with conventional ones because the two categories of IT will inevitably need to work together when deployed. In the last decade, the stovepipes of isolated IT applications have given way to systems and infrastructure that are interdependent. Projects as novel as Intel's ergonomic advising software, for example, must be fitted into Intel's standard desktop environment.

We are not saying that centralized innovation with pipelines containing only innovative projects are impossible. We are saying that the path from an innovation being a research finding, leading to a workable idea by a pathfinder (i.e., basic research) and onward to an innovation ready for the development group needs to be well marked. The centralized scenario requires close communication, management of expectations, and understanding of the production environment that lies at the end of the pipeline.

Open versus Closed Pipelines.   In the case of IT innovation, it is difficult to imagine an entirely closed innovation pipeline. The reason is that so many innovative tools are immediately available that accelerate the IT organization's work. Every make-versus-buy decision is a choice between the open and closed approach and certainly a modern IT organization would leverage existing products rather than recreate them. In our view, bringing outside innovation into the pipeline at the engineering step is always a good idea.

The more interesting question is whether and when to send ideas out of the pipeline for others to license. Intel IT and Intel Corporation have a strong commitment to externalization of ideas in nearly every case. The exceptions are for enabling technologies that are fundamental to Intel's core business, such as device physics and manufacturing process technology. Intel IT holds several patents and, as a matter of practice, licenses its innovations to third-party developers.

Step 2: Capture Innovation Ideas

Innovation ideas can be derived from several different functions in the company and with several different methods. One rich source is the IT support staff. Incident tracking systems identify recurring problems where innovations are needed. They reveal the nature of the problem as well as the people who are spending time away from work struggling with an IT issue. In some cases, support is needed, but in other cases an investment in improving an IT capability is in order. For innovation in general, product returns and customer complaints provide a similar source of innovation ideas for products and services provided to customers outside the company. While well-running IT systems can be improved, we have found that solving problems with innovation pays back handsomely.

A second source of ideas can be drawn from emerging technologies that offer new functionality. In 2005, for example, early adopters began reporting a variety of applications using radio frequency identification (RFID) technology. A standards body emerged as competitors worked to make sure that interoperability was assured. Vendors and consultants began showcasing new or improved IT capabilities based on RFID. IT suppliers began offering off-the-shelf systems for generic tracking needs and IT consultants began proposing RFID extensions to their clients.

The population of IT users is the final source of ideas. If asked and reinforced for answering, IT's customers have a lot to say. In addition to problems that are tracked by support systems, these customers have suggestions for improvements or perhaps blue-sky ideas. New hires from other companies bring with them different IT experiences, perhaps even from different industries. Harvesting these ideas is a worthwhile effort.

Step 3: Create and Populate a Registration System

A pipeline registration system stores ideas with descriptions in a repository that is a database of innovation raw materials. Intel's Innovation Engine provides a simple registry of innovation assets that accepts input from global Intel employees as well as our business partners. Our portal allows innovators to enter a description of their idea, their names, and to state the type and maturity level of their proposed innovation.

The result is a searchable pool of raw material for innovation projects. We have found that existing sources of innovation—online document libraries, R&D archives, technology development databases, internal conference papers and web sites and product group monthly status reports—can often be mined to avoid having to start from scratch. While mining assets is time consuming and requires dedicated resources and tools, it is a good source of ideas. Mining also helps locate experts who can evaluate innovation ideas and thus is an efficient way to build the expert and prototype developers pool.

An even more productive way to build an idea asset pool is by using campaigns to harvest ideas, needs, or challenges from individuals, teams, and communities. The Innovation Engine was designed to provide this functionality. Here are three examples from Intel:

- In 2006, Intel IT campaigned for ideas that would improve IT efficiency. Templates provided by the Innovation Portal are available to make posters quickly and consistently. We provide links to marketing and communication so that our campaigns appear in company newsletters.

- In anticipation of our first dual-core processor release, Intel polled employees and trading partners seeking usage models. With more powerful processing technology, in what new ways would our customers put our product to work? Employees provided over one hundred ideas.

- Intel has a technology strategic long range plan (T-SLRP). In anticipation of an annual update, the T-SLRP team campaigned with the question, "What next-generation technologies should Intel be investing in, and why?" This campaign generated over four thousand ideas, a four-fold increase over the prior year.

We found that our first campaigns were too open-ended and lacked focus. Having an open-ended asset capture system is rather like having a suggestion box. The ideas that spring from it can be so diverse that the effort required to evaluate, manage, and drive them to an end value is far greater than when a campaign is focused on a particular topic. With a topical campaign, we can identify our experts in advance and schedule them for vetting sessions.

Campaigns are contests and there is a winner—the best idea of the lot is identified and the person submitting that idea is rewarded. One reward is the opportunity to attend an Intel Developer's Conference, a privilege that most Intel employees do not have. And we also offer technology gadgetry, which is especially popular at Intel.

Step 4: Choose a Vetting Procedure

The vetting process for campaigns relies on a committee of experts who understand the technology issues for a campaign. This transfers the burden of vetting to people who are best equipped to judge the ideas. In the case of usage models for dual-core processors, the expert team was formed from several different business units and included an author of this book. We wanted the widest array of expertise possible. The committee divided ideas into three categories:

- Ideas that were infeasible, and thus set aside. And, as expected, we did receive some usage models that would be impossible to support.

- Ideas that were already in use, albeit in rarified environments. This category was surprisingly large and highly informative. Collectively, our employees were aware of a number of niche applications that could become mainstream with the dual-core processor's capabilities.

- The third category contained ideas deemed innovative—new, useful, and possible. Many ideas in this category were quite creative and, after some deliberation, we identified a winner. Using one core for multimedia and the other for processing was the winning usage model. The idea came from an Intel account representative who was not a member of the IT organization.

On Ice

Much to the frustration of innovators, there is a history of innovations that are ahead of their time. While the innovator has a vision of something new, further exploration reveals that the barriers to creation or adoption are simply too high. Wise innovation managers archive these ideas so that they can be revisited at a later time.

Video chat is a classic example. Doug Engelbart invented and demonstrated the video chat concept in the 1960s, far in advance of affordable personal computers and available bandwidth. In our terms, Engelbart's system was a concept car.

Intel delivered the ProShare™ camera collaboration tools in the 1990s and once again the technology failed to diffuse. When the internet provided backbone bandwidth, the last mile adopted DSL and Data over Cable, and video cameras became less expensive, then video chatting became a reality.

Step 5: Manage the Innovation Project Portfolio

While innovative IT projects are tracked and stage-gated along with conventional IT projects, we do gather them into portfolios and we manage them more aggressively to mitigate risk. Innovations are new, and thus there is no history from which to draw lessons. And, the portfolio of innovative IT projects allows for different development paths. For example, if engineers believe that an innovation cannot be fielded for a generation or two, then it may be held in archive or the innovation may be expressed as a concept car (see sidebar).

Other innovation projects may be vague and in need of refinement. In considering the deployment of wireless mobile technology at Intel, for example, we invested time in ethnographic studies to observe user behavior and in experimental studies to estimate productivity gains (Intel 2004).

Business cases are needed before a project launches into the engineering stage, and that is another facet of portfolio management. Our six-vector management model shown in Figure 3.2 on page 36 highlights the possibility that an unfavorable business case may call for us to change our vision and develop a new prototype to test a different technology solution.

Finally, when we manage the portfolio of innovative IT projects, we remain willing to stop some projects, accelerate or decelerate others. While conventional systems follow a more predictable route and ordinarily deliver a necessary system, we find that innovative projects are more volatile.

■ Accelerators include activities among our competitors that favor one project over another or larger-than-expected benefit estimates emerging from prototyping experiments.

■ Decelerators include the need to reallocate resources to a high-priority project or the discovery that a new technology component is not as mature as expected.

■ The most common reasons we stop a project are timing and a radical change in business value estimates, which are often related. At stage-gates, we re-examine the business value and cost estimates and reconsider ROI.

For example, we sometime conclude that a delay of a year will bring lower cost, higher performance, or greater maturity to a component technology and that change will tip the scale in favor of progressing. We archive the project so that we can jump-start the effort in the near future.

By archiving the halted projects and reinspecting their status regularly, we ensure that a halted project is not a failed project to be discarded, ignored, and forgotten. There is much to be learned when prototypes fall short of expectations.

According to McNichol (2007), Google embraces a *fail-fast* approach. McNichol describes Google's method as *launch, listen, improve, launch again*. Innovative IT projects are experiments and should be conducted as efficiently as possible. Scientists and IT innovators can both learn a great deal from projects gone awry.

We offer one final suggestion regarding portfolio management. Diffusing too many innovative IT capabilities rapidly for a community of users can quickly lead to adoption fatigue. We aim to pace the delivery of innovations and we think in terms of a collection of S curves spread across time. (See the The S-curve Perspective on page 135.) For a community of users, innovations that require training are best spread out over time.

Adoption Fatigue and Tolerance for Interruption

Adoption fatigue is caused by too many changes in the environment and will lead to rejection of innovations. Many of us dread the release of a *new and improved* product because we know from past experience that learning the differences takes time and can be quite frustrating.

Another barrier to adoption for some IT innovations is the level of tolerance people have for interruptions. For self-healing systems or tacit systems, the level of interruption can be higher than some users are willing to tolerate.

When one is working studiously and absorbed in a task, the IT solution that interrupts that process one too many times will be turned off or uninstalled. Examples of interrupting IT solutions include automated upgrades and patches, email compression utilities, and instant messaging—especially the latter.

Step 6: Establish and Use Value Realization Metrics

During the pipeline management process, a collateral effort is needed to develop and test business value dials. (See Business Value Dials on page 25.) For innovative applications, new or modified value dials may be needed. And, baseline measures will be critical when assessing the impact of a new IT capability.

Former CEO, Andy Grove, is well known for coining the phrase, "If you can't measure it, you can't manage it." As a result of his dictum, Intel has a wealth of metrics that are already in place. Measures of intermediate quality permeate our fabrication processes. Our e-business systems monitor raw materials and finished products closely. And our planning processes demand measurable objectives.

We cannot overstate the importance of establishing metrics, especially for innovative IT projects. Finance and business managers remain skeptical of IT activities and they often argue that IT innovations are solutions looking for problems. To succeed over time, the IT organization must demonstrate a problem-solving approach with business value metrics expressed in monetary units.

Improving Yield for IT Innovations

We closely monitor the innovation pipeline itself. Here are some of the metrics we use to obtain quarter-over-quarter trends in IT innovation activities:

■ Success of innovation campaigns is measured by the number of campaigns, the number of ideas submitted during the campaign process, and the yield, that is, the number of ideas accepted for implementation.

■ At Intel, when an innovation occurs, the innovators file an invention disclosure form. These forms are evaluated by legal and technical experts. We track the number of forms submitted and, again looking toward yield, we also track the number of innovations routed onward to be patent filings, preventive publications, or trade secrets.

By preventive publications, we refer to the practice of publishing ideas to establish prior art and eliminate the risk of a patent filing from another company. Look to online forums such as www.ip.com for more information.

■ We count research and development proof points to see how many ideas are translated into working systems with a usage model and a simulation or a prototype. Proof points are demonstration systems that show which ideas are viable and better communicate a vision of an innovative IT capability.

■ We track the proportion of awards (i.e., rewards and recognition actions) given by the company for IT innovations. We believe that awards are an important part of systemic innovation because they celebrate those who take the risk to suggest and develop new ideas. We also actively monitor awards outside the company. These events indicate overall industry leadership.

■ To monitor diffusion, we keep an accounting of IT innovations that move from early adopters to the early majority, that is, innovations that cross Moore's chasm. These IT capabilities sometimes diffuse actively using our copy-exactly methodology and in other cases, are adopted by individuals downloading the application from our early-access portal, the IT Innovation Zone. A final measure of diffusion is the number of IT innovations that move into widespread usage virtually instantaneously. The adoption of wireless network technology at Intel is an example.

Tactics for Improving Yield

Our overall strategy for IT innovation pipeline management is expressed in our model's stages and value paths. Here are some more specific tactics we have found useful to ensure that innovative ideas receive appropriate attention and support, and that IT investments lead to breakthrough solutions, new products, or better business practices.

- Engage with IT architects and capability managers early in the development process to ensure readiness for adoption when the innovation has matured.

- Examine the company's product lines and operations to understand critical business and technology needs, influence roadmap direction, and the selection of innovation pipeline candidates.

- Maintain effective representation in relevant business decision-making forums and cultivate ongoing discussions with business managers.

- Capitalize on thorough planning, development, and deployment to influence outcomes and to capture the business value of innovation-initiated projects.

- Adopt a learn fast, fail fast strategy, that is, complete a cycle of rapid prototyping, discard what does not seem useful, and advance the results with the most potential. Disney and Google both espouse this approach.

Sample Results

By defining the end goal and grounding every innovation in a business need, innovation pipeline management can set forth a roadmap for keeping innovation and research investments clearly focused and delivering maximum value.

During 2006, at Intel IT, thirteen projects emerged from the lifecycle pipeline and moved into production. Some examples include:

- A Business Value Capability Maturity Framework (BV CMF) workshop — a comprehensive and practical training class in IT value management for CIOs. The workshop is delivered as a part of our Innovation Center activities.

- SKuBA— an application that provides better sharing of real-time factory information from a fab back to designers. SKuBA helps to deliver better products and eliminates the need to perform several revisions of a new product when it is being introduced.

- The IT Innovation Zone (ITIZ) — an early adopter innovation distribution channel and virtual community for cutting edge tools leveraging web 2.0 and social software. Inputs to the pipeline can come from within an IT department, within the company, or from an external sources.

Intel Innovation Index

The metrics that we created to measure our innovation program evolved over time into a numerical innovation index. Of course, metrics vary by company and depend on the company's business model and strategic objectives. At Intel, our Innovation Index contains the following elements:

- Innovation Campaigns—the number of topics IT or Intel as a whole requests input using the innovation engine.

- Ideas Submitted—the number of innovations submitted during the campaign process. This index item indicates the level of participation in the organization and helps identify innovators for specific topics.

- Ideas Accepted for Implementation—the number of innovations surviving expert review that are approved for further investment.

- Invention Disclosure Forms (IDFs)—the number of application forms completed by innovators for formal IP protection. These forms are reviewed by our legal department and internal industry experts.

- Invention Disclosure Forms approved for Patent Filing, Publication, or Trade Secret—a yield function to monitor the IDF function.

- R&D Proof Points—the number of ideas that are translated into a proof points having a usage model, simulation, or prototype that better communicates the vision and is used to explore the idea's viability.

■ Innovation Reward and Recognition—the number of awards issued related to innovation. We use an internal reward and recognition system with tools to track awards to reinforce innovation in our culture. We also apply for external innovation awards to demonstrate our innovation leadership in industry.

■ Crossing-the-Chasm Innovations—the number of innovations that are adopted and put to use by employees either informally, using our portal to download unofficially supported tools and processes, or formally, using our copy-exactly diffusion methodology.

■ IT Hero Products—innovations that are adopted internally by the enterprise and end up becoming part of business-unit or enterprise builds or are published and shared externally to our industry via www.itsharenet.org. (We use the term *hero products* in place of *killer applications* which, while common in the industry, has negative connotations.)

■ Innovation Assessment Score—the score from the innovation assessment that indicates the organization's innovation maturity.

Summary

In this chapter we addressed the issue of pipeline management for innovative IT projects. We offered different pathways to value and identified the stages in the pipeline. We shared with you our heuristics for maximizing yield and minimizing risk. Our take-home message is that innovative IT projects require keen management attention which, when applied, bring them into the IT product lifecycle and into adoption.

Chapter 8

Diffusion of IT Innovation

*Getting a new idea adopted, even when it has
obvious advantages, is difficult.*
—Everett Rogers

Diffusion is the active dissemination of proven good ideas.
The term is borrowed from chemistry and physics, where it describes
the random distribution of molecules in a medium over time. A drop of
ink in a beaker of water diffuses over time until the entire beaker is evenly
tinted. Innovation diffusion can occur randomly over time as new products and services, like molecules, move through social networks.

However, we believe that the diffusion of innovative ideas need not be
random or accidental. In fact, it can be deliberately directed, managed,
and accelerated within an organization. This can be accomplished especially in IT organizations, because the IT organization is in a position to
promote and market its products to its IT customers to accelerate usage.

In this chapter, we review the academic foundation of the concept of
innovation diffusion in some detail, beginning with Rogers's (2004) foundation and ending with Freedman's thoughts about a flattened world. To
these theoretical analyses, we add our insights and experience at Intel
and provide a sequence of steps for systematically diffusing IT innovation
throughout an enterprise. The more rapidly an innovation diffuses, the
more quickly we can measure business benefits and report the return on
our IT investment.

Diffusion Fundamentals: How Innovations are Adopted

Used as a metaphor to explain how new ideas become widely adopted, *diffusion* has referred in the past to the dispersion of new ideas through social networks. Everett Rogers, originally an agriculture major at Iowa State University, achieved academic fame for his theory on innovation diffusion, published in his book *Diffusion of Innovation,* now in its fifth edition (Rogers, 2003).

Categories of Adopters

When Rogers collected data on adoption, he found that very few people took on an innovation when it was first available. Over time, uptake increased, peaked, and then the rate of uptake slowed and eventually just a few people jumped on board and the market for the innovation was saturated. To make contrasts among these adopters, Rogers needed categories and so he turned to statistics and made an assumption common in science, which is that a normal distribution described his data.

■ In a normal distribution, 68% of the population lie within one standard deviation of the mean. As shown in Figure 8.1, Rogers named the 34% to the left of the mean as the *early majority* and 34% to the right of the mean as the *late majority.*

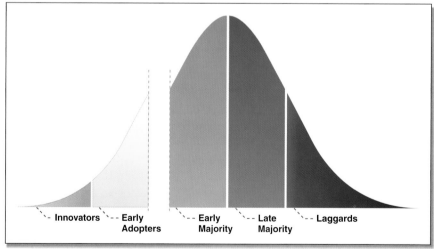

Figure 8.1 Adoption Concepts from Rogers and Moore

Source: Adapted from Rogers and Moore

- Rogers named the next 13.5% of the population who adopted an innovation before the *early majority*, those between the first and second standard deviation in a normal distribution, to be *early adopters*.

- And for that 2.5% of the population to first adopt an innovation, those beyond the second standard deviation, Rogers adopted the name *innovators*.

- After the late majority, those 16% beyond the first standard deviation from the mean Rogers labelled *laggards*.

These statistically-defined categories allowed Rogers and many other researchers to collect data on adoption and to contrast the characteristics of named subgroups in a consistent manner. Over many years of research, Rogers and colleagues studied diffusion of innovation using these categories.

These investigators found that willingness and ability to adopt new ideas is dependent on awareness, interest, and experience, and people could fall into different categories for adopting different ideas. A farmer, for example, might be quick to accept the idea of hybrid corn, but be a very late adopter of the iPod. We encourage IT innovators to read the fifth edition of *Diffusion of Innovations* (Rogers 2003), as it contains hundreds of thoughtful insights relevant to many industries and contexts.

The Chasm

In 1991, Geoffrey Moore used Rogers's normal distribution classification scheme to illustrate a particularly difficult transition in the diffusion of technology innovations. First, Moore combined innovators and early adopters into a single group named for the latter. Next, Moore speculated from his experience coaching technology start-up companies, that products entering the marketplace had a particularly difficult time satisfying the needs of both early adopters and the early majority.

Moore observed that early adopters were technology enthusiasts and risk-takers seeking a radical shift in technology capability. These highly-skilled adopters were willing to work with incomplete products—raw material, if you please. The early majority, in contrast, wants a whole product, a complete solution, and an easily understood implementation process.

Moore paid special attention to a gap in the graph that he identified as the *chasm*, as shown in Figure 8.1. The chasm was the point of greatest risk because young technology companies were pulled in two directions—to increase complexity and serve the early adopters or to increase simplicity and serve the early majority.

Successful new technology suppliers take the latter tack. Highly successful technology suppliers have woven the chasm assumption into their product development lifecycle. In the world of R&D, researchers share results with early adopters, and developers build for the early majority.

Chasm Two

Moore is focusing his attention on the gap between early adopters and the early majority because he studied where good ideas can get stuck when they are departing from the development stage. In our experience, there is a second gap of which innovators should be cognizant. This is the gap between innovators and the early adopters, as shown in Figure 8.2.

Problems at this transition are aggravated by companies that compartmentalize their research and development processes, we believe. And it will be the pathfinders who collect the discrete ideas from innovators and inventors and assemble them into a more organized collection of ideas that attracts the attention of the early adopters.

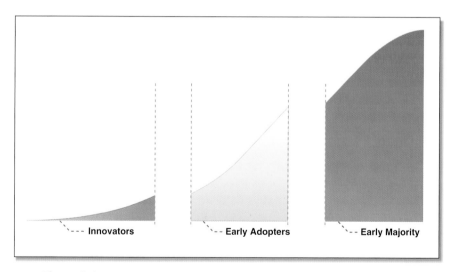

Figure 8.2 The Second Chasm

Source: Intel IT, adapted from Moore, and Rogers

The S-curve Perspective

If we accept Rogers's normal distribution assumption and plot that distribution as accumulated adoption over time, an S-curve results, as shown in Figure 8.3. The S-curve perspective highlights how adoption accelerates when the early and late majority begin to adopt.

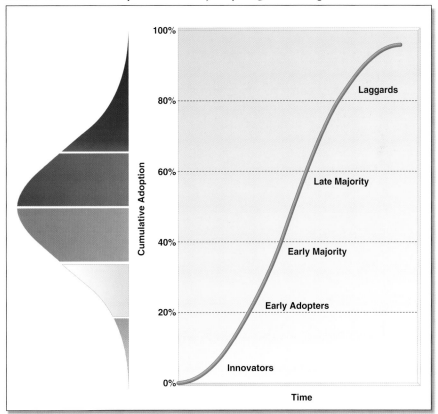

Figure 8.3 Cumulative Adoption S-curve
Source: Rogers (2003)

In an active and innovative IT organization, a family of S-curves will describe diffusion over time. Figure 8.4 illustrates the lessons learned from multiple S-curves. We are assuming that 100% is the total population of the company. Here are the lessons:

■ As shown by curve A and curve B, not all innovations diffuse at the same rate. When plotting several diffusions, some will rise more quickly and flatten out sooner. This is especially true for IT innovations. When an operating system upgrade goes out to every PC, the S-curve is nearly vertical, as shown by curve C. Elective downloads may diffuse for weeks or months.

▪ When 100% is the total population of the company, not all innovations reach all members—nor should they. An IT innovation for the marketing group may never have usage by engineering whereas desktop innovations may impact nearly everyone in the company. Factoring in the total available market is important for IT innovation managers.

▪ As signified by the ⊗ at the end of cumulative curves in Figure 8.4, all IT capabilities are eventually decommissioned or brought to the end of their lives. The life span of an innovation is yet another

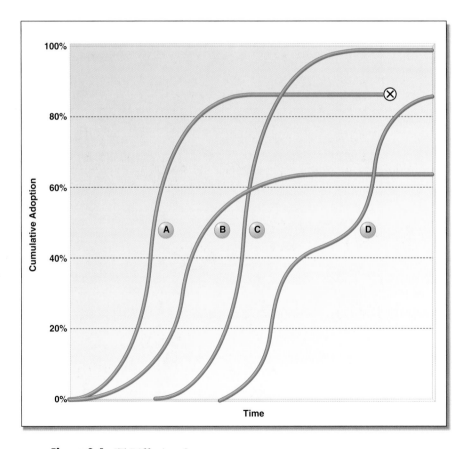

Figure 8.4 IT Diffusion S-curves

Source: Intel IT

variable for IT innovation investment managers to consider. It is highlighted by an S-curve analysis.

■ Most large-scale diffusions are staged with the cumulative curve revealing releases in different departments, communities, or geographical areas, as shown by curve D. Scientists and statisticians agree: Beware of the normal curve and the S-curve because they are idealized functions.

Metcalfe's Law

Metcalfe's law states that the value of a network grows with the square of the parties connected. Formulated by Robert Metcalfe, co-inventor of the Ethernet, this law has been used to explain the adoption rates for communication technologies, networks, and internetworks (e.g., the Internet). The corner cases are illustrative.

■ If someone had the only telephone in the world, to whom would that person place a call? A network of one produces no value.

■ If everyone had a telephone, then all parties are within reach. A network of all produces the greatest value.

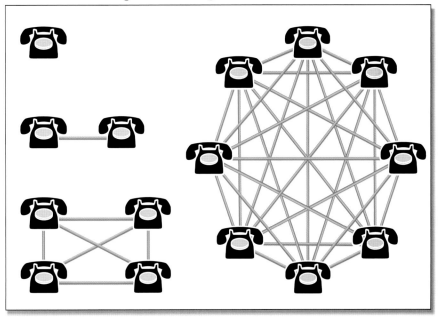

Figure 8.5 The Basis of Metcalfe's Law

Source: Adapted from Wikipedia Public Domain

Metcalfe's law—the rule that value grows with the square of the number of networked users—is illustrated in Figure 8.5. Interconnections grow as a square of the number of nodes. Metcalfe's law, taken literally, produces a curve that soars to a maximum value as the population of users is exhausted. Figure 8.6 illustrates the curve as value rises to 1,000,000 when networked people increase to 1000. We say *literally* because there is a debate in the literature as to whether Metcalfe's law is to be taken literally. Metcalfe does not define a metric for value, which is part of the problem, and there is some debate about whether $Value = People^2$ is the correct mathematical function.

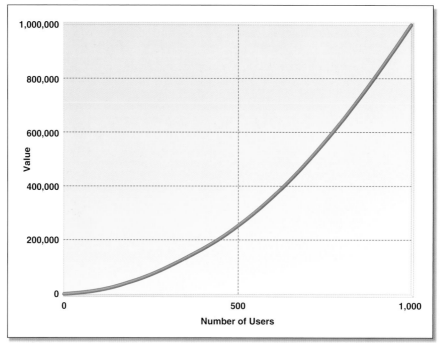

Figure 8.6 Number of People and Value of a Network

Source: Intel IT

Gladwell's Tipping Point

Malcolm Gladwell's studies of diffusion focus on the special roles that some people take as ideas spread through a community and on the explosive nature of change when a critical mass is reached. That critical mass is *The Tipping Point*, which is also the title of Gladwell's first book (Gladwell, 2000).

Connectors and Mavens

Gladwell's thinking begins with his realization that some individuals are able to muster more support for a new idea than others. In a social network, not all people are equally powerful. Using a sociological test, Gladwell identified what he calls *connectors*—individuals with very large social circles. These individuals are especially capable of delivering strong endorsements for new ideas to a large group of people.

In thinking about our own colleagues and friends, we can easily identify connectors. They not only stand in line overnight to purchase the first of a new model of consumer product, they are also the people who let everyone know about that product and how valuable it is.

To complement the connector, Gladwell also posited the role of *maven*. Mavens are the men and women who deeply understand the complexities of a market or a technology. In our world of IT, a few of the industry analysts have emerged as trusted advisors about the current and future trends in the technology marketplace. And, among colleagues and friends, we have those trusted advisors that we turn to when we want a quality opinion or judgment.

According to Gladwell, actively identifying and combining mavens and connectors into teams is a powerful way to effect change. Reliable and respected information can be widely broadcast in a relatively short period of time. Mavens guide connectors who are the largest hubs in the social network.

The Tipping Point

It is Gladwell's observation that change, which in our context is the adoption of an innovative IT capability, begins slowly as word gets out that something better is available. As more and more people adopt an IT innovation, the rate of adoption begins to rise. Much in the spirit of Rogers, Gladwell believes that a tipping point is reached and the adoption of change then occurs very rapidly.

Friedman's Flat World

In 2005, Thomas Friedman published a book about how converging technologies were changing the nature of global business. Friedman's allusion was to a flat, fair playing field where modern countries and emerging ones could begin to do business. Of the ten *flatteners*, four are emerging information technologies. Friedman highlights the browser, workflow software, informing, and personal digital equipment. By informing, Friedman means the use of search engines like Google to independently gather information. Underpinning these flatteners is the internet.

These new technologies and the internet together change the way companies work together. These five flatteners are open sourcing, outsourcing, off-shoring, supply chaining, and insourcing. Friedman's example of insourcing is UPS, who in addition to its delivery services, provides repair services for Toshiba computers.

Friedman emphasizes that the world is flat because of the convergence of these technologies and business models. For knowledge-based industries, the relationship between where work is needed and where it is done has vanished.

Diffusion Fundamentals: Lessons Learned

We have offered ideas from five distinguished individuals who have looked at diffusion in slightly different ways; Rogers, Moore, Metcalfe, Gladwell, and Friedman. From our diffusion practitioners' point of view, here are the implications we have drawn for our daily work:

■ From Rogers we acquired shared terminology and an understanding that, over time, diffusion will begin slowly with innovators and early adopters. The concept of tracking multiple S-curves over time has helped us to understand variances in diffusion. Some IT capabilities have a higher velocity uptake, for example, and when looking at an organization as a whole, S-curves top off at different levels.

■ Moore's contribution to our thinking centers on the chasm. When IT organizations develop and field innovative IT capabilities, their first customers are those early adopters who treasure function over simplicity. Listening solely to these customers can lead to a product that is unacceptable to the majority of our customers. The remedy, of course, is to build prototyping and testing programs that draw on the larger population of customers early in the development process. In this way, the risk of falling into the chasm is lessened.

■ From Metcalfe there are two messages. The subtle message is that an expensive network infrastructures will not be cost effective if usage is low. Economies of scale are an important consideration when building a business case for an innovative IT capability. The bold message is that the benefits of network systems rise sharply as the number of users increases. Linear increases in cost-per-user will quickly be outrun by quadratic increases in accumulated benefits.

■ From Gladwell we learned that you can push a rope. Namely the random diffusion process that describes molecular behavior need not be random when diffusing new IT capabilities. Identifying mavens and connectors is a useful exercise for diffusion managers. Expediting access to innovative products and services for these types of individuals is a viable technique for accelerating adoption of IT innovations and innovations of all kinds.

■ Friedman highlights the consequences of a global internet with useful tools such as browsers and work flow systems. For some companies, the work of innovation can be and is being brokered and dispatched to contractors and suppliers anywhere on the globe. For diffusion managers, the internet provides a pervasive and inexpensive way to send out new IT capabilities for testing and, later, for daily use. Friedman also suggests a new world where innovations can be customized for individuals, and in the flat world, diffusion channels can be bi-directional and return information from customers' experience with a new product or service.

Diffusion of IT Innovation

The goal for diffusion is to obtain maximum penetration of the IT innovation in the desired end user community with the least amount of investment. If active efforts to accelerate diffusion are not taken, a valuable innovation will be adopted slowly or, perhaps, not at all. Proactive steps should be taken to develop infrastructure, provide technical support, and actively market the innovation, as shown in Figure 8.7. Well-managed diffusion with discipline enables efficient distribution and faster return on investment.

The mindset for IT diffusion managers should be one of marketing a product. Technology products often emerge from the engineering department with a host of features. These features need to be transformed into benefits to attract the interest of IT's customers. Similarly, functions fulfill needs and skilled marketeers find ways to fit a new product into the customer's daily life. Usage can be demonstrated in many ways. Live demonstrations, Web demonstrations, and case studies are three of many ways to reveal the product's value to the customer.

Assets, Methods, Skillsets

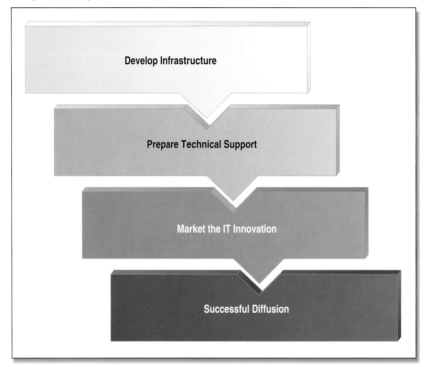

Figure 8.7 Steps in Managing IT Diffusion
Source: Intel

When we think of strengthening our diffusion capabilities, we sort out assets, methods, and skillsets that we have or need. We form a framework, as shown in Table 8.1, and look at their alignment with the diffusion steps from Figure 8.1. We call this a *directed* diffusion framework to underscore the fact that we are actively diffusing innovations, and not simply waiting for the social network to do so.

Develop Infrastructure

The infrastructure that supports directed diffusion draws on assets, methods and skillsets.

Assets

Like any well-run business, the IT organization needs to think through and develop distribution channels to deliver IT capabilities. A part of this asset is always in place—its basis is the network that integrates our IT systems and is the distribution channel of choice for software.

Table 8.1 The Directed Diffusion Framework

	Develop Infrastructure	Prepare Technical Support	Market the Innovation
Assets	• Delivery channel • Innovation centers and portals • Content repository	• Toolkits for support • Courseware • User's Guide	• Audience analysis • Marketing expertise • Publicity assets
Methods	• Embed innovation into existing systems • Use an intranet innovation portal • Copy-exactly	• Recruit experts • Test the innovation repeatedly during development • Develop training for all stakeholders	• Brand clearly and consistently • Align messages to business goals • Exploit both Web and paper media
Skillsets	• IT expertise • Innovation expertise • Diffusion expertise	• Technical writing • Instructional design • Product support personnel	• Marketing and communications • Mavens and connectors • Media developers

Source: Intel IT

Innovation centers provide focus and the opportunity to demonstrate IT innovation, both within the company or to the outside world. Innovation portals augment the center and allow remote workers, trading partners, and customers to look in on our new ideas.

The innovation portal can also be a one-stop shop that supports innovation at large. The portal can be a gateway to innovation web sites, tools, reward and recognition systems, applications for funding, and idea-capture sites. At Intel we include organizational information related to innovation. For example, we have a section for champions that has information to assist with delivering innovation to their organizations.

Methods

Innovative IT capabilities can often be diffused by building them into existing systems. And many IT innovations manifest themselves as extensions to software that is already in use. IT's customers will find it easier to explore a new feature than to assimilate an entirely new application.

For client-side innovations, it may be possible to fold the new capability into the operating environment. Most IT organizations standardize a build for all personal computers, update it, and upgrade the user community on a regular basis. IT innovations can ride on the shoulders of this process.

For personal computer innovations that do not necessarily affect all of IT's customers, a download service is useful. Our ergonomic software discussed in chapter three was distributed in this fashion. Some innovations are best offered on a discretionary basis. Also, users can then choose a quieter time to load them and learn them.

Server-side innovations should exploit the advantages of a Web interface when at all possible. Browsing is a process our customers are familiar with. The more we can make customers comfortable with the IT innovation, the better it will diffuse.

We remind the reader that we believe strongly in the advantages of the copy-exactly process. For customers and to reduce costs, it is far better to over-invest in developing a high-quality IT capability and then diffusing exact copies of it far and wide. Conversely, incremental releases of an IT innovation to different communities, poor quality, and local tinkering leads to unhappy customers and outrageously high maintenance costs.

Skillsets

Three specialties converge when building innovation infrastructure, IT expertise, innovation expertise, and diffusion expertise. Someone is needed who understands the existing IT architectures and standards. Innovation expertise includes user-centered design skills, human factors experience, and ethnographic capabilities. In conjunction with these players, the diffusion expert can plan for and build the needed infrastructure.

Prepare Technical Support

The next step is to create technical support for the pool of innovations currently in the pipeline that have been developed to the point of being able to deliver value through communication.

Assets

For most IT innovations, toolkits will be needed for the product support organization. In many ways, this community comprised the early adopters for the innovation. Product support personnel need to understand the use of the innovation and, in addition, they will likely need to know more than the average customer about configuring the innovation and solving typical problems.

Courseware may be required and a user's guide showing the innovation in action is helpful. Investment in these diffusion elements varies with the costs, risks, size of the customer audience, and complexity of the IT innovation. Courseware developers, like product support personnel, are excellent beta testers as they work to construct an orderly presentation of the innovation's functionality.

Methods

When the IT innovation prototype is up and running, showing it to content experts is a good idea. If, for example, a new Web-based. zero-based budget system is under development, then we recommend demonstrating the system to a Web wizard and a zero-based budget wizard. Gaining approval from these experts can be part of the marketing effort.

Testing IT innovations must be relentless. The copy-exact mantra, *make the first one perfect*, applies here as well. The IT organization must build a reputation for quality as well as innovation in order to succeed. Diffusing anything less than a well-tested system puts more than the innovation at risk, it puts the IT innovation opportunity at risk.

Skillsets

Technical writers, instructional designers, and product support personnel are needed at this stage. Access to the IT innovation prototype is crucial. We expect the innovation project team to include people with these skills in every case. In other words, we do not send a specification to the technical writing team, we place a technical writer on the innovation team.

Marketing Innovations

It is at the marketing step that our IT organization looks most like a business. We advertise, we make sure that features are translated into benefits. We offer the IT equivalent of a test drive around the neighborhood.

Assets

While innovation developers are concerned about usage models and user-centered design methods, the marketing group wants to understand the customer as well. Who makes the buying decision for optional IT innovations? What criteria are most important? A careful analysis of the customer's buying habits is crucial to successful diffusion.

The IT organization at Intel has a dedicated marketing group. These are professionals who know how to conceptualize and package IT solutions as attractive products and services. They understand the importance of branding and positioning when reaching out to customers.

By publicity assets, we mean the capability to put together marketing campaigns and product launches. For Intel IT, this translates into templates for posters, Intel IT graphics libraries, and booths for demonstrations and road shows.

Methods

Branding is not usually a part of the traditional IT organization's thinking, but it looms large in the minds of customers. Over time, brands deliver the reputation of the product or service offering. Our IT Innovation Engine is a good example from our work. The name loads up the features and values of the service and delivers them to our customers.

Innovative IT applications should have been aligned with company goals and objectives when the business case was created. These linkages are the basis for another marketing vector. IT's customers need to know why the company is investing in a particular innovation and what business value benefits are expected.

While it is tempting to use Web-based communication exclusively to reach out to IT's customers, we have found that traditional paper-based communication is also important. A eye-catching poster in the coffee room, an article in the company's newsletter, and a full-fledged advertisement will all help accelerate diffusion.

Skillsets

Preparations for the market launch bring two new skillsets to the innovation team. A marketing and communication person is needed to create a brand image, a positioning, and benefits-oriented descriptions of the new IT capability. The team also needs a media developer to re-express the marketing communication packaging and advertising. For software products that display an interface to the customer, its signage and color should be a part of the marketing plan.

We discussed the roles of Gladwell's mavens and connectors earlier. Well before the product launch, we identify, approach, and invite these these individuals to look in on the developing IT system. When connectors are assured by mavens that the IT capability will be important, then the word will begin to spread around the company that something interesting is in the works.

One Final Ingredient for Success

Diffusion can be enhanced by the reward and recognition systems that support innovators both in IT and especially in the company at large. This has been an effective part of diffusing the IT Innovation Engine at Intel. Contests with rewards and recognition communicate the company's interest in innovation. When winning ideas emerge in different functional areas of the company, employees outside of R&D and core business services will participate.

Summary

We have offered four key ideas about diffusion:

- An invention that diffuses rapidly will accrue business value more quickly. From a cash flow point of view, this is a good thing.

- An invention that fails to diffuse cannot deliver business value. Inattention to the diffusion process is a recipe for failure.

- Innovation theorists think about diffusion in different ways, each of which provides insight and guidance.

- Diffusion can be accelerated. We call this *directed diffusion* and we have provided a framework filled with ingredients for building this capability.

And remember, don't defuse innovation, diffuse it.

Chapter 9

Launching Systemic IT Innovation

Innovation distinguishes between a leader and a follower.
—Steve Jobs

This final chapter brings together all the themes in our book and offers a plan for building an innovation program in the IT organization. Much of the innovation activity will result in better IT systems for the company. Some of the innovation activity will support innovation excellence across the company.

Innovation is crucial to meeting the challenge of balancing today's IT operational excellence with future needs and managing for business value. In order to stay ahead of the competition and contribute to shareholder value, innovation needs to be systemic. It provides the company with a critical ability to adapt to changes in the business environment.

The path to innovation excellence begins with management commitment. Employees need to know that innovation is on that short list of capabilities that the company must have. They must perceive that being innovative is the best way to move ahead in the company and the best way to help the company move ahead.

The IT organization is well placed to cultivate innovation capabilities, both internally and across the company. These capabilities are a mixture of courses and workshops, methods and metrics, and systems to manage the innovation process. Over time, investments in innovation enablers will establish innovation as an enterprise value.

Gaining Management Commitment

Commitment from management is an absolute necessity when launching a company-wide effort of any kind. It is the responsibility of the company's executives to set forth a strategy and to identify the key capabilities which will enable the company to thrive. Capabilities may include an emphasis on quality, a goal of being first to market with new technologies, or a reputation for using IT in innovative ways throughout the company. Top-down support begins the journey from random and occasional innovation to systemic, methodical innovation.

Managers demonstrate their commitment by sending clear and visible messages that innovation matters. In addition to rhetoric, management commitment includes concrete actions such as allocating resources, putting innovation metrics in place, and paying ongoing attention the innovation process. When upper management puts innovative excellence on the middle manager's list of objectives, then we can rest assured that middle managers will be communicating that same message to line managers and employees. Each workgroup manager is responsible for the day-to-day details of implementing or participating in an innovation program.

Create and Communicate a Vision

A vision is a view of the future that emphasizes what a company intends to accomplish. Vision is important because it paints a picture for the entire organization and sets expectations. Moreover, the differences between the state of the company today and the vision of the company in the future translate into a roadmap of accomplishments needed to satisfy the vision.

In May of 1961, President John Kennedy declared to the US Congress and the American people that he intended to send a man to the moon and safely back within the decade. This bold statement galvanized efforts by NASA to engineer a solution to Kennedy's challenge. Kennedy did not say that space travel would happen some day and that we would go somewhere. It was a manned flight to the moon and back, we have nine years to do it, and the clock starts now. In July of 1969, Neil Armstrong set foot on the moon.

The best visions are concrete, specific, and challenging. They translate well into slogans and are memorable. They electrify emotions and create cohesion in organizations. A well-crafted vision statement sets the company thinking of where they are and where they need to go.

Visions are typically formed on the basis of forecasts. Gordon Moore's 1965 extrapolation of early trends in the density of semiconductor devices provided our industry with a yardstick, on the one hand, but more importantly, with a new set of questions about the future. What if we could create a device with 50 million transistor junctions? What would it do? How would that device fit into a system? What other components will be needed?

To be effective, the company vision must be widely communicated and reinforced over time. The company's employees, customers, and suppliers all know what to expect. A well-communicated vision creates a spotlight of attention. When that spotlight is focused on increased innovation, the stage is set.

Develop an Innovation Strategy

The next step in launching an innovation initiative is to develop a strategy. For innovation, or any other objective, the first step is an inventory of relevant current assets and capabilities. Depending on the organization, this step could be complex. Like quality and safety, innovation capabilities can be difficult to identify and quantify. Especially in the case of skillsets, it may take some time and effort to find out who has experience with innovation techniques.

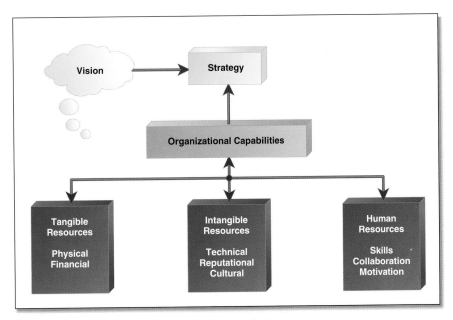

Figure 9.1 Vision, Strategy, and Capabilities

Source: Adapted from Robert M Grant, Contemporary Strategy Analysis Competency Model, MacDonough School of Business, Georgetown University.

A strategy maps the company's capabilities to the vision, as shown in Figure 9.1. A strategy is the roadmap that leads from today's capabilities to the capabilities needed to support the vision. The roadmap has a timeline and a sequence of milestones to measure progress. While long-term planning may reach out a decade or more, preparing three year action plans and revisiting those plans annually is typical.

Budget intersects with strategy as well. Especially in the IT organization, there are many investment alternatives. Weighing those options and testing how they align with corporate objectives is a key activity. Finding the right balance between innovation and operational efficiency occurs at this juncture.

Outcomes vary up and down the organization. Corporate visions and goals translate into greater detail until they find their way to specific action plans for each employee. Managers create projects, form teams, and monitor progress. In the case of innovation, new outcome measures (i.e., business dials) may be needed.

Measure Business Value

A sustained commitment from upper management will depend upon measured business results. CEOs are measured by the value they create. Stockholder value increases with the company's measured performance. Thus, if innovation initiatives are not explicitly tied to business results, then they will quickly lose the attention and support of upper management.

We call our metrics business dials, and a sampling of dials is given in Table 9.1. For each dial, we define how value is going to be measured. Financial dials are rather straightforward. We want to see more revenue, or perhaps more revenue while holding the profit margin constant. We aim for fewer days of inventory and fewer days of receivable. Everything is in monetary units.

Indirect financial dials are a bit more difficult. For example, the simple number of patents should increase when systemic innovation programs are launched. But how much is a patent worth? It is our objective to transform the indirect business dials into monetary units, and that can be a significant challenge.

Table 9.1 A Selection of Business Value Dials

Indirect Financial Dials		Direct Financial Dials	
Intellectual property	Patents	Revenue	Days of inventory
Standards influence	Product influence	Days of receivables	Headcount
Sales influence	Vendor of choice	Productivity	Turnover
Usage models	Prototypes	Risk management	Scrap reduction
New markets	Business process	Factory uptime	Time to market

Source: Intel IT

Developing Innovation Capabilities

The inventory of innovative resources, created as a part of the strategy process, provides a foundation for developing additional innovation capabilities. As always, there are interdependencies among the choices. We suggest an incremental and balanced approach, with investments in tangible resources, such as an innovation center, along with human resources, such as people trained in user-centered design.

Training

In the early phases of an innovation initiative, we typically see the need to invest in training. Large corporate IT organizations often have training expertise in place, and can add courses to an existing curriculum. In smaller companies, the IT organization may choose to budget for outside training, which exists in abundance in the area of innovation. We identified some elements of our training courses when talking about innovation capabilities.

As innovation skill sets improve and experience accumulates, we recommend that the IT organization provide courses company-wide. Since innovative activities vary in different industries, courses can be tailored to the company's specific needs.

Attending innovation conferences is also helpful at the onset. Conferences accelerate the open innovation process by displaying a number of successful innovations, often in different industries. Conferences also provide a setting for a company's innovation program manager to network with other managers.

Steps to Integrate Innovation into the Company

1. Review all job descriptions and add innovation as an expectation.

2. Review training and development support systems and identify existing courses that need to support innovation.

3. Create an action plan to update existing materials and release to the organization.

4. Source the innovation gaps through make-versus-buy decisions.

5. Provide 24x7 access to training materials, both virtually and physically where possible.

6. Develop innovation competency measurement tools.

7. Provide time and space for experimentation.

Sophisticated innovation programs should consider sponsoring an innovation conference. Most commonly, these events are by invitation and provide a splendid way to include suppliers and customers in the innovation process. Publicity related to the conference will enhance the company's reputation for valuing and cultivating innovation.

Reinforcing Innovation

Along with training, early plans for launching an innovation program should include methods for reinforcing innovative behavior. In a nutshell, we celebrate success and we learn from failure. We begin with the more difficult case.

Learning from Failure

How an organization reacts to failure is a good indicator of how successful an innovation program will be. Traditionally, failures are punished, and yet we all recognize that innovation is a risky business. If potential innovators in a company observe bad outcomes when a project founders on unexpected rocks, they will be unlikely to step forward when a new project is launched.

As mentioned, the best failures are those that occur early in the development process and that provide useful information. At Intel we call this *failing forward*. Ideally, we would like the first-order prototype to reveal as many problems as possible. User-centered design is helpful in this regard. We avoid the temptation to go away and build what we think might be needed. We test early and often, throughout the development and adoption processes.

At Intel we bring projects to closure by identifying and archiving lessons learned, both positive and negative. This process brings closure to the team and encourages the fact that all projects provide value. Knowing what does not work, what does not work *yet*, and what does not work for us is valuable information. When the results are archived, we celebrate the achievement.

Celebrating Success

We recommend strong reward and recognition systems to celebrate successful innovation. Intel's systems for reward and recognition include a mix of financial and non-financial reinforcers, which we also recommend. Reputations matter and recognizing an engineering team for delivering on deadline and to specifications is a powerful reward. Meanwhile, if an innovation can be linked to improvements in business value, then we believe compensation is appropriate.

Rewards need not be substantial in all cases. Offering a trip to a conference for the 100th person to file an idea is a good way to encourage innovative thinking, for example. Providing a convenient parking place for the inventor of the month chosen by election among peers is another modest example.

Innovation Centers

Dedicating a space to support the innovation process raises the visibility of the innovation program. One or two rooms will be needed to support workshops and demonstrations, which are the most common usages for innovation centers. Early on, the IT innovation center may be little more than a setting for evaluating new technologies, demonstrating concept cars and prototypes, and offering workshops and training courses. Most activities will be within the company, with an occasional visit from a vendor or customer.

In conjunction with an innovation center, we recommend an on-line virtual innovation center be created. In the early days, the virtual innovation center will contain course listings, calendars of events, and links to relevant resources. Later on, the virtual innovation center can become a portal in support of innovation in the large. Systems like our IT Innovation Engine can automate the capture and management of innovative ideas from all around the company.

As momentum increases, innovation centers will likely reach outward to include activities designed for customers, suppliers, and other interested parties. Although they manifest themselves in different ways, these centers make sense for any knowledge-rich industry. Here are three different types of innovation center:

- PricewaterhouseCoopers (PwC), the global business advisory partnership, created a technology center in the mid 1980s. The research center developed practice aids to accelerate the audit process. In addition, the center also served as a destination for visits from CFOs. PwC wanted to demonstrate to its customers and prospects that it was committed to streamlining the audit process.

- Procter and Gamble (P&G), the consumer products company, added the Beckett Ridge Innovation Center in the year 2000, bringing the total number of innovation centers to six. These centers provide visions of the future packaging and use of home products. Also, P&G features innovation at its Web site. Through a program called Connect+Develop, anyone can submit a product or technology idea to the company. (www.pgconnectdevelop.com)

- AXXIS Technology, a regional IT services company serving New South Wales, Australia, and a winner of the Australian Business Council Award for Innovation in 2006, uses its own IT systems as sales tools when approaching small and midsize businesses (SMBs). AXXIS is itself a midsize business and SMBs often have no IT personnel. Thus the selling process is primarily by demonstration with AXXIS providing systems and support. When AXXIS integrated mobile devices into SMB client-server systems for their own use, they also created exactly the demonstration needed to show to their customers.

These three examples show that innovation centers will vary in focus and scope to support different corporate visions in different industries. For PwC, innovation was focused on practice aids whereas for P&G, the focus is product development. We include Axxis Technology to underscore the point that innovation centers can be portable and that there are many opportunities for SMBs, and those who serve SMBs, to be innovative.

Creation and Diffusion

When launching an IT innovation program, we recommend choosing early projects with special care. While it is tempting to propose a risky

Criteria for Siting an Innovation Center

As Intel IT expanded its collection of IT Innovation Centers, we formalized our criteria for choosing a new site. Here are our primary heuristics:

- Geography—Our objective is to distribute the innovation centers to provide global coverage.

- Intel presence—We want our centers located near the majority of our people.

- Customer presence—We want to be near our most important customers.

- Local support—We are influenced by requests from employees, customers, and suppliers who want an innovation center nearer to them.

- Innovative culture—We favor sites that are near universities, institutes, and other research and development facilities.

- Optimum cost—We favor locations where we can share costs with other innovation programs, receive contributions from local governments, and put idle resources to use.

Like many collections of heuristics, some of these are at odds with others. Thankfully, our virtual innovation centers do reach every corner of the world.

idea that might be a smashing success, we suggest the safer bet—a project that reapplies a trusted IT innovation in a new setting. Costs and risks are lower, providing a much lower hurdle for success.

"A common expression of wishful thinking is to base a grand scheme on a fundamental, unsolved problem," according to Gene Glass (Glass 1978). Wishful thinking and innovation are a dangerous mixture. In IT, startup ventures often bring grand schemes to the IT organization's attention. Beware of the concept car that is promoted as a prototype, or even worse, as technology ready for deployment.

Partnering and prototyping are the keys to managing risk, as shown dramatically by our case study of Wireless Westminster in Appendix A. This strategy is not just for beginners. We at Intel IT regularly develop cooperative ways to include partners in our innovation projects. Because successful scaling is a well-known challenge for IT systems, we are careful to deploy prototypes in realistic environments.

Getting the diffusion strategy right is equally important. While legacy research on innovation highlights random adoption in a social network, we believe that diffusion can be actively directed and accelerated, especially for IT systems. The incremental cost of supporting additional users is ordinarily low and, as a result, the more rapidly we can deploy innovative IT capabilities, the more rapidly business value will accrue.

Intel's Experience

When Intel IT began to focus on innovation, we had a substantial inventory of resources. This is not surprising, given the nature of our core business. What we envisioned was a day in the future when IT systems would expedite innovation across the enterprise. That is, while building new and better IT capability was one of our primary objectives, we also wanted to build the infrastructure for innovation *writ large*.

Our investment in innovation centers is significantly large, in proportion to the size of our company and to their importance to our strategy. The centers are distributed globally and comprise executive briefing facilities, prototyping capabilities to test emerging technologies, and regular programs in which we share IT best practices with ourselves and with our customers and suppliers.

Innovation Enablers and Inhibitors

In 2004, Intel IT conducted a workshop attended by employees from across the company. One result from that workshop was an ordered list of enablers and inhibitors, which is shown in Table 9.2.

We suggest planning an innovation launch strategy with this table firmly in mind. While it is impossible to eliminate all inhibitors, we believe it is helpful to identify them clearly and construct work-around tactics. For example, if an innovative IT project depends on new enabling technologies and lacks an ironclad diffusion vector, then it may make good sense to argue for a longer ROI payback period. Or, in that same setting, an additional prototype may be needed to verify the expected return.

Table 9.2 Enablers and Inhibitors of Innovation

Enablers	Inhibitors
1. Management support—active and positive support for innovation from the top down	1. Bureaucracy—too many approval steps to launch a new initiative or expand on an idea
2. Employee talent—a pool of employees with diverse skills and abilities and the confidence to use them	2. Negative leadership—innovation not supported at a high enough priority to carry projects through
3. Rewards and recognition—ongoing positive reinforcement, including tangible rewards when appropriate	3. Immediate ROI—expectation that an innovation will provide a return on investment in too short a period of time
4. Open communication—open door policies and a community that values the sharing of ideas	4. Risk aversion—simple avoidance of all risk without weighing the opportunity cost of inaction
5. Competitive pressure—the healthy stress of staying ahead of competitors with new and better ideas	5. NIH syndrome—not invented here blocks the adoption of good ideas learned elsewhere
6. Access to resources—sufficient and sustained budget to fuel the innovation process	6. Too little time—day-to-day responsibilities exhaust available bandwidth
7. Risk taking as a value—the thoughtful balancing of opportunity and risk to maximize benefit	7. Organizational protectionism—barriers within the company that block the sharing of good ideas
8. Policies that support innovation—workshops, release time, mentorships, innovation centers, etc.	8. Lack of funding—lean resourcing of people and funds that reduces the opportunity to innovate
9. Job rotation—the opportunity to gain and share ideas in different settings within the company	9. Lack of vision—no clear picture of where the company will be in the future and thus no path to get there
10. Innovation platforms—systems and repositories for the intermediate results of the innovation process	10. Fear of change—believing that work should be done like we always have, with legacy systems, not innovations

▇▇▇▇ Systemic Innovation

We recommend the control-loop approach to managing and improving IT innovation capabilities, which we introduced in Chapter 4. Business-like thinking, a carefully-managed budget, increasing IT innovation capabilities, and assessment of the results are the critical functions, as shown in Figure 4.1 on page 53.

Systemic innovation will not be an overnight success. It will take several trips around the control loop for IT innovation managers and the company as a whole to understand the process, its requirements, and its benefits. We suggest that launching an IT innovation program will take two to three years. In terms of the IT Innovation CMF, moving up a step each year is a reasonable expectation.

Innovation at Intel in the People's Republic of China

Intel's Pudong PRC Site leadership team recognized the importance of innovation and co-funded an innovation center and an innovation program in 2004. The program began with completion of a self assessment and grew in maturity over time. Construction of the innovation center was completed in 2005 at a cost of approximately $50,000. In 2007, the innovation team completed a manufacturing improvement project that finance estimates will return $6.3 million over two years.

Culture and Innovation

It is our contention that when innovation is cultivated, it will become systemic, which is equivalent to saying that innovation will become a part of the company's culture. Culture comprises people's shared beliefs and values. Culture shapes how people normally behave and interact in their daily life and in their work environment. The concept of corporate culture encompasses far more than dress codes and cubicles. The most important part of corporate culture is the shared commitment to company values, for example, to quality, safety, and innovation.

Summary

Launching a systemic innovation program presents interesting challenges. We intended this chapter to identify the paths forward and the potholes to be avoided. Our major advice is as follows:

■ Gaining and maintaining management support remains at the top of our list of concerns. We shared our experiences with creating a vision, developing a strategy, and measuring business value.

■ We outlined the major elements needed to begin developing innovation capabilities. To ascend the levels in our IT Innovation CMF, training will be needed and incentives must be in place to reinforce innovative behavior.

■ We believe strongly in the value of an Innovation Center, especially in support of corporate-wide innovation. We also believe that the exact nature of the innovation center's charter will vary by industry and company size.

■ We shared a top-ten list of innovation enablers and inhibitors based on workshop findings at Intel.

■ We returned to our foundation thinking about systemic innovation to remind and recommend the control loop approach to running IT innovation like a business. We suggest repeatedly attending to innovation business, budget, capability and impact and making improvements at each turn of the cycle.

Stay in touch

We will be posting innovation material on our book's Web site. Register your book and stay in touch.

Case Studies in IT Innovation

Innovate and integrate to work smarter, not harder.
—Dan Etheredge, Intel Corporation

There are few reports of the challenges faced when identifying, developing, and diffusing innovative IT capabilities. At the same time, there is an abundant supply of white papers and news releases that report on successful IT innovations. Thus we know where to go, but not always how to get there. We offer two case studies focused on the process of delivering innovative IT capabilities.

- The City of Westminster is a borough in the heart of London and its governing authority has for many years been intent on providing excellent public-sector services. Could IT be used to better support mobile service providers such as parking enforcement officers? Would a wireless investment pay off?

- At Intel, significant resources are dedicated to supporting IT systems and often the support is provided by help desk personnel. Could some of the support features be expedited by IT systems and, if so, what are the candidate support functions? An overall model for support is needed.

The authors express their appreciation to the innovators who shared their experiences with us and our readers.

Wireless Westminster, Part 1

"I believe that it is time for us to push our service excellence to the next higher level," Peter Rogers stated. Rogers, Chief Executive of the City of Westminster, was discussing strategy with the Leader of the Council, Sir Simon Milton in early 2003. Sir Simon Milton was clear that the Council needed to develop a vision for the city that delivered world-class services efficiently and effectively on a 24 x 7 basis and needed to embrace the many constituent communities—residents, businesses, and visitors. This later became enshrined in the Council's One City vision.

The City of Westminster

The City of Westminster is a borough in the heart of London. It is home to over 200,000 residents and also to the seat of government for the United Kingdom. Embedded in a Greater London metropolis of 17 million people, the City of Westminster supports a diverse population far greater than its resident population. Over a million people join the City's residents on a daily basis. Commuters flood into the City to work in its many businesses. Theatres and concerts bring many more, and visitors to London seek out destinations in the City such as Hyde Park, Piccadilly Circus, and Buckingham Palace and the night spots of the West End.

Vision

Rogers asked for input from two of his staff, Vic Baylis and Graham Ellis.

"To be aligned with the Council's agenda, we should seriously consider a vision for actions that will reduce crime," Ellis suggested. "We know it's a problem, most often caused by criminals who are not residents of our City and also by the opportunities created with the many late-night activities in London's West End. And. we must work to coordinate our needs with a police force that is London-wide."

"With fewer police on the beat, we have a scarce resource that is not capable of being everywhere," Rogers added. "We need to find ways to support the policing resource and to increase its efficient use. And, the police are one of several street-based resources. We have parking wardens, noise monitoring personnel, and people who inspect and provide permits for various functions in the City."

"Mobility is a common element, isn't it?" Baylis observed. "We should focus our thinking about how we can reach out to our mobile workforce, direct them to where they are needed, and provide them with access to information when they are on the streets of the City. We have an opportunity here to allow them to work more smartly and to enable them to spend more productive time out and about in the City rather than wasting time travelling back and forth to the office."

Innovative Uses of Information Technology

One of Westminster's elected Councillors, Ian Wilder, was first to see the potential benefits of using wireless technology to support the Council's vision. It was Wilder who saw wireless technology in its infancy in the United States and introduced Rogers and his team to the pioneering work being done by Intel at the time.

"When mobility is an issue, wireless networking comes to mind," Vic Baylis said. "The demonstration systems we observed at Intel certainly suggest that this technology is robust and ready to deploy. And, industry analysts agree that wireless network technologies will be increasingly important in the future."

"Imagine what we could do if we could deploy our camera capabilities without cabling," Ellis suggested. "The sheer cost of cabling is an inhibitor to that effort. With a wireless network, we could deploy cameras to an event or to a street within hours. That would be a massive improvement on the months it was taking to redeploy cameras on the existing fixed-line network. This would result in far more dynamic and flexible enforcement model across the City not only for the Council but with its key enforcement partners, notably the Police.

"If we plan for sufficient bandwidth and work with the right partners to construct a truly city wide network, then we might also be able to 'piggy back' other applications and offer access to our City's residents and businesses," Baylis added.

"A Wireless Westminster," Rogers concluded. "Please take this vision and build it out further. We'll need a small proof-of-concept prototype system. We will need to examine two primary benefits, one for improving security with wireless cameras and the other to optimize the mobility and productivity of our staff on the streets. And, our Council will certainly want to see a robust business case."

The Prototype

One way to test a technology's maturity is to see what others have learned. Westminster City capitalized on Intel's investment in an IT Innovation Centre in Dublin, Ireland. A visit to the Centre provided Rogers and his team the opportunity to see wireless technologies in use. Intel had recently developed and delivered a campus-wide wireless infrastructure and it was adopted rapidly. Intel's studies of the business benefits of mobile computing enabled by wireless networks showed significant paybacks in monetary terms.

"Our experience with mobile systems enabled by wireless networking leads us to believe that the technology is robust and ready for deployment," said Martin Curley, Intel's director of IT Innovation. "We began our prototyping about two years ago. Uptake by operating groups at Intel has been quite rapid."

Usage Models for the City of Westminster

"The visit to Intel's Innovation Centre was helpful," Peter Rogers noted. "It's time to think more specifically about our mobile workforce. We want to avoid the tendency to create solutions looking for problems. What we need is a winning application—an application for which there is a compelling business case."

For Westminster, one winning application might be the administration of parking in the City. There were approximately 250 street wardens walking beats in the City. The blend of wireless cameras that could be moved around without any fuss and more intelligent deployment of the street wardens offered a new parking enforcement model across the City. It meant the number of street wardens could be reduced because camera surveillance allowed monitoring from a central site and with the right technology provided the prospect of streamlined administration and reduced handling costs of all the *back office* processes.

The flexibility of wireless technology also offered new opportunities to relocate the administration centre to cheaper parts of the country. Baylis saw the main benefit being a very different model for city management, moving away from traditional *beats* or inspection regimes to one which facilitated intelligent deployment of street-based resources across all public services

"Let's assume we have an incident at Leicester Square." Vic Baylis said. "With our cameras, our street-based staff can receive real-time streamed images on their hand-held device, assess the situation and dispatch appropriate resources—City guardians, wardens, or the police. We can see whether weapons are involved and whether anyone is injured."

Prototype Phase 1.   This thinking led to a first prototype, designated Phase 1A by the innovators. A single key component of the overall vision, wireless camera technology, was deployed at Soho Square and tested for 30 days. To reduce risk and to begin building strategic partners, the City of Westminster teamed with Vertex, an outsource provider of IT services. Intel Corporation, Cisco Systems, Telindus, and Capgemini also joined the team. By December, 2003, the first prototype had delivered a technical success. The City could reliably monitor activities with cameras supported by a wireless network. And the functionality was so useful that the system was not turned off.

Prototype Phase 1B. Following the successful technology proof-of-concept experiment, the City of Westminster launched a more complex second prototype, which was designated Phase 1B. Phase1B was a 3-month experiment that extended beyond camera technology to see how well other applications could be supported for different City workers and services. These other applications were aimed at suppressing crime and anti-social behavior, monitoring noise, supporting mobile devices for parking wardens and food and licensing officers. Vic Baylis and the Council's IT organization proposed to expand the system to include a wider Soho area, and importantly, two large housing estates, Lisson Green, and Churchill Gardens. Both were under the management of the Council's arms-length housing company called CityWest Homes.

Westminster and Vertex IT strategists also wanted to better understand the integration of camera technology and mobile devices to provide an integrated street management system. And, most importantly, Westminster needed to generate empirical benefit estimates to support a business case for full deployment. The Phase 1B prototype investigates benefits for mobile workers as well as the wireless cameras. Would an investment in Citywide wireless networks improve the City's ability to serve its residents, businesses, and visitors?

The Business Case

For the City of Westminster, the outcome metrics of interest are not the typical business-value indicators such as profitability or market share growth. Along with cost reduction, a significant improvement in the quality of public services was paramount to enhance its reputation as a world-class city. At the top of the list of concerns was safety.

In late 2004 the City Council considered an expenditure of £1.293M to fund the Phase 1B prototype. To justify the investment benefits were identified in four key areas:

■ Improved public security and safer street environments. Remote monitoring with cameras would target anti-social crimes such as flyposting, refuse dumping, and illegal parking.

- Increased productivity and efficiency of mobile workers. Licensing inspections could be recorded electronically and transmitted to the City's IT systems instantly.

- More intelligent deployment of street based staff leading to new models for integrated street management across a broader range of services. Scarce resources could be directed to areas of need with information gained from the camera network and transmitted to the mobile staff.

- Opportunities for residents. The same network that supports City services would also be available to residents to move to on line transactions with the Council—particularly in the area of *payments*.

The £1.293M would be the City's contribution to a total cost of £2.527M. The City had stakeholder contributions and a government innovation grant totalling £1.527M. Vertex offered to contribute half the cost of developing the new applications and CityWest Homes contributed funds to extend the Phase 1B to include some of its properties.

What should the City of Westminster do?

▐ Wireless Westminster, Part 2

Following Council approval, Phase 1B was launched within 12 months. As hoped, British Telecom (BT) joined the collaboration, which reduced cost further. BT's interest was in piloting for-fee WiFi services and the Phase 1B experiment was a perfect test bed.

"We're seeing some challenges," Vic Baylis told Graham Ellis, as they monitored deployment of the system. "Development of the mobile applications for food and licensing officers is lagging, and we won't have findings in Phase 1B. Camera reliability is another concern. And how different functions share the camera resources is more difficult than expected."

"Remember that we're the first City in the world to experiment on this scale," Ellis replied. "And the problems that are emerging are surmountable. Our phased approach to prototyping covers these snags."

Phase 1B went into operation and between December 2005 and March 2006, the project team monitored the indicators previously selected against pre-determined baselines. That is, the team compared *before and after* surveys of residents and local business.

Business Process Changes

"Many of our expectations are being realized," Peter Rogers told Vic Baylis and Graham Ellis as they pored over the empirical data. "Look at this. For parking, the blended *camera-and-street-warden* model resulted in less wardens on the street being more productive than before. One side benefit which had not been anticipated was markedly less violence against the wardens from aggrieved motorists. Sound monitoring, while not fully deployed, is also showing potential to help in the enforcement of our licensing conditions for restaurants, pubs, and clubs."

"Experiments on our housing estates through CityWest Homes were quite revealing," Baylis pointed out. "CityWest has concluded that the wireless technology, per se, does not positively impact their ability to respond to needs for repair. They found the cameras useful, and expect them to be a substantial means of combating crime and disorder at their housing estates." This was endorsed by the residents of Lisson Green estate, who noticed a big improvement in their quality of life.

CityWest and other parts of the Council also concluded that they would need to change their business processes to gain more benefits from the wireless systems. This has been a common finding over the years when new technologies and existing business processes come together.

Organizational Changes

The UK Home Office recommended that Phase 1B findings for crime and disorder reduction be anecdotal, rather than statistical because three months does not provide enough data to uncover robust trends. Meanwhile, the effects of the wireless capability did change the way in which the policing agencies did their work.

First responders were more able to move to trouble spots and the wireless camera capability was directly associated with 58 incident responses, 15 arrests, 5 victims taken to hospital, and 20 police stops where police question suspects at the scene.

Societal and Customer Changes

In April of 2006, Peter Rogers looked over survey results for residents in the Phase 1B areas. "Residents reported that they were pleased to see more parking attendants," he noted. "And, in fact we have reduced the number of attendants during that time. Our efficiency in this domain increased in a visible way. Our service was also seen as fairer—a good result when paying fines is never going to be popular."

"Residents also report that they feel safer with more cameras in place," Graham Ellis added. "More residents are noticing the cameras and also noticing that we have more of them. Except for some early concerns with health risks and wireless networks, acceptance in the community has been positive."

"While residents see the cameras, they don't know that the WiFi is there." observed Vic Baylis. "In one way this is a good thing because they shouldn't have to care about what technology it's based on, but in another way we have a really exciting opportunity to engage our residents and communities about what else this technology can do and what other applications we can run over a wireless network."

Vision Revisited

"The results of our 1B prototype are quite encouraging," Peter Rogers declared. "And, with these experiments, we have a much sharper vision of how wireless and mobile technologies fit our needs." Figure A.2 shows a refined vision of how the wireless City benefits its constituencies in different ways.

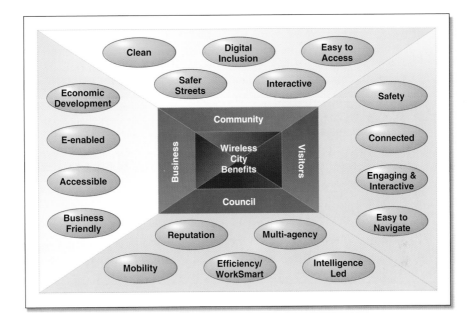

Figure A.1 Usage Models for Wireless Westminster

Source: City of Westminster

Epilogue

Based on success of 1B, in November of 2006 the Council approved a plan to build a wireless network across Westminster in collaboration with Vertex, Capgemini, BT, and Telindus. Westminster is the lead UK city in BT's Wireless Cities Programme and in the autumn of 2007, BT is about to complete a square mile of wireless coverage across the West End of London.

The first wave of Westminster's private network is complete and the City of Westminster is now successfully using wireless CCTV for wider enforcement including parking. Final testing is underway on other mobile wireless applications to follow and a pioneer competition has been launched to engage residents, neighborhoods, businesses, schools, and visitors in coming up with additional ideas. For more information, see *www.wirelesscitypioneers.com*.

Innovative eSupport at Intel, Part 1

"These projects, however clever, are just not lasting over time," Dan Etheredge reflected as his next assignment was on the horizon in 2003. In his role as an IT support engineer, Etheredge had built a half-dozen or more software tools to expedite product support. Scripts, help files, FAQs—a collection of useful information for IT's customers and for IT support personnel. However, as assignments shift, these homespun materials and tools fall into disrepair and disuse.

"Let's do some thinking about how support systems could be improved," Etheredge said to Mark Storace, then the technical manager of the IT group's call tracking system. "We need an overall framework to understand how support systems fit together. Independent 'point' systems simply aren't effective."

In reviewing the literature in search of new ideas, Storace and Etheredge came across a Forrester Research (1999) model that offered both a view of the state of the art in e-support systems and also a view toward the future. That diagram is shown in Figure A.2. Influenced by internetworking, Forrester analyst Paul Hagen postulated that a new and more efficient tier would soon appear in customer support systems.

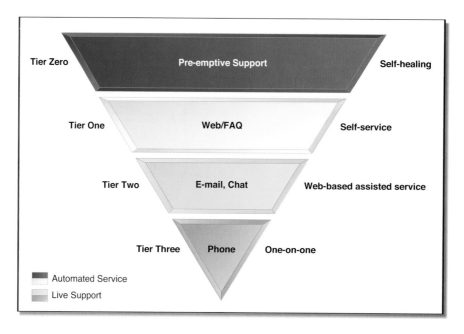

Figure A.2 Four Tiers of Support

Source: Forrester Group, 1999

A Vision is Born

"This Forrester model makes a lot of sense," Etheredge said to Storace. "The Tier 3 method for helping customers is one-to-one contact between a support person and the customer, and this tier identifies the most expensive way to provide support. Tier 2 solutions are web based and allow a support person to address the needs of several people at once, using email or chat capabilities. Tier 1 solutions provide FAQ and knowledge bases so that customers can find solutions for themselves. And to these three layers, Forrester has added a fourth: Tier 0 methods preempt the need for support by automatically healing the problem, perhaps without the customer's knowledge."

"Forrester's inverted triangle highlights two important issues," Storace pointed out. "First, progress up the layers demands increasingly sophisticated technology and a deeper understanding of potential support needs. However, with each step upward, the cost of support decreases dramatically. This is most clear with Tier 0. When we broadcast updates across a wide audience of customers, we are preempting a multitude of recurring problems."

"There are two other important lessons here." Etheredge added. "These support systems have broad applicability. If we were to develop a well-engineered infrastructure for our IT support needs, that infrastructure would be available to others at Intel who provide support of different kinds. HR has a multitude of needs, for example, that are primarily inside Intel. Purchasing has another set of needs, both within Intel and including Intel's trading partners.

"The second lesson is that vendors in the packaged software market are gaining maturity. We have been building point solutions because we had to. It's time to consider whether we can buy and configure systems, rather than building custom solutions. While the content of our support systems will be unique, the requirements for storing, retrieving, and delivering support are likely to be very similar to other enterprises."

Formalizing the Effort

Polly Herren joined the effort in 2004 and took responsibility for evaluating the business implications of the technology alternatives. She worked with Dean Wehsels, who focused on the technology itself. Intel IT is methodical about its choices of software products and Herren and Wehsels applied their methods to available support system solutions.

"We focused on the functionality currently available in the products we evaluated," Herren explained. "What might be available in the future was set aside. We also examined the ability of products to integrate with existing Intel systems, for example, our ActiveDirectory and our personnel databases. The goal was to find a software platform that was ready to be configured to our needs and to avoid software platforms that would need to be customized.

"We also asked for reference accounts and spoke with other IT organizations in larger companies like ours. Then, when we narrowed the field to two companies, we invited them to spend a week with our support organization and demonstrate how their products could be configured to our needs.

"We performed a careful analysis of how an eSupport system would be deployed at Intel and what business benefits we could expect to counterbalance the costs of development and support. We needed to consider how the system aligned with the company's overall strategy as well," Herren concluded.

All of this work culminated in a business case for an investment in a third-party software product providing innovative tools to automate customer support. The business case looked at gains in efficiency as tasks are migrated higher in the Forrester's four-tier model.

"The bottom line of our business case was that, over time, we could increase the quality of support while, at the same time, reducing head count." Herren explained. "Moreover, again over time, we could re-invest some of the resources freed up by our more efficient eSupport systems, and with technology improvements, we could strive to move our support procedures higher in the Forrester tier model."

Calling for the Question

In 2003, the eSupport project sponsor, Ron Hurle, took the team's plans before Intel's IT Business Process Steering Committee and to Doug Busch, Intel IT's CIO. As Hurle explained it, "When it comes to providing customer support, we are currently in a stove-pipe mode. What we need is a single, solid eSupport strategy." eSupport was positioned as part of a larger Intel IT goal: to reduce the unit cost of delivering current IT services by 50 percent and to free people and dollars for investments in new competitive capabilities.

The eSupport team forecast a 35% reduction in the cost of support achieved in the second year.

Should Intel IT invest in eSupport?

▐▬▬▬▬▬ Innovative eSupport at Intel, Part 2

With endorsements from management oversight committees and from IT's CIO Doug Busch, the eSupport project was approved and the project kicked off in early 2004.

"We involved our customers early in the process," Herren explained. "We knew that user acceptance of new support systems would be a critical factor. We put measures in place to track system usage and to locate areas where support was weak or unsuccessful. We built marketing material to inform our customers what we planned to do and when to expect changes."

Initial Development

To plan an order of attack, the eSupport team inventoried existing support technologies and identified which new capabilities would make the most difference early on. The vendor providing the packaged software, *SupportSoft*, also provided advice on which capabilities to launch first.

ServiceDesk "In the initial deployment the *ServiceDesk* capability was called *AskTech*, and that was a mistake." Herren explained. "It was a hard word to say and to hear. A lot of people thought the system was *Aztec*. And so early on we renamed the overall eSupport system to be *ServiceDesk*, and that worked much better. *ServiceDesk* is a multi-channel user portal that is the gateway to our eSupport capabilities."

Tier 1 *KnowledgeCentre* was the first capability delivered by way of *ServiceDesk*. This capability provides IT's customers with ways to help themselves via *tell me*, *show* and *do it for me* scripts. They were created in the format of Frequently Asked Questions (FAQs) with the "do it for me" scripts also having embedded links to solutions that customers could directly execute to resolve known issues on their PCs themselves.

Tier 2 *LiveAssist* (or CHAT as it was initially named) was deployed next and provided real-time access to service personnel using a web based instant messenger interface as an alternative to phone support. In the Forrester model, this capability is at Tier 2. With both parties online, service personnel could show the customer where to find necessary information or provide it directly. More importantly, one support person might well be helping two or three people at the same time, which is a gain over the one-on-one characteristic of telephone support.

Tier 0 The third key capability deployed was *PC Health Check*. This capability was a Tier Zero application capable of preemptive, automated support. As the name implies, the system was capable of identifying and repairing problems with personal computers. "Since the potential leverage was so great for this service," Herren said, "we spent extra time thinking about how we might best deploy it."

Diffusing PC HealthCheck

In 2006, the eSupport team prepared to launch *PC HealthCheck*. To make sure that their customers were aware of the new offering, the team planned a series of roadshows. eSupport teams visited Intel sites in Chandler, Arizona; Beaverton, Oregon; Swindon, UK; Dublin, Ireland; and Chengdu, China.

"We provided demonstrations of *PC HealthCheck* and supplied our customers with fact sheets and a success story white paper." Herren said. "We also listened carefully to what our customers had to say about PC HealthCheck in particular and about IT support resources in general. Several customers had ideas about how we might improve *PC Health-Check*. Adding the capability to verify security settings was one of those ideas."

Effects on Work

"eSupport improved employee career paths for our group," Herren reported. We still utilize people delivering advice by phone, but now those people can move upward to provide Live Assist Chat. With more information being captured about support requirements, there are now positions for support analysts—people who study the support process and seek out incremental innovations."

Also, as a global company, Intel has a multitude of employees for whom English is a second language. Providing self-help in a written form and interactive help as a chat session actually eases the way for the non-English speaker. This applies to both support personnel and the IT customers that they serve.

Customer Consequences

"As we continue to study our customers' satisfaction, we've found that our self-help systems are empowering. When we provide the right information and the ability to search for what is needed, people are able to serve themselves. This is the Tier 1 approach." Herren explained. "In fact, I have a report from a customer:

> *ServiceDesk is an awesome resource! I was having an issue and I typed in a few words and performed a search. I*

scanned the returned results and voila! Your tool provided the info I needed! Saved me much time! Love this tool! Thanks!"

Business Value Consequences

Measured results in 2007 show that the eSupport function requires 14% fewer people—a direct cost avoidance benefit. What is more difficult to measure is the time saved for IT customers who can more quickly, proactively, and efficiently maintain their PCs and remain "on task" with their daily work.

An Evolving Vision

As eSupport capabilities continued to roll out, Etheredge and Herren revisited the original Forrester figure that had jump-started their thinking.

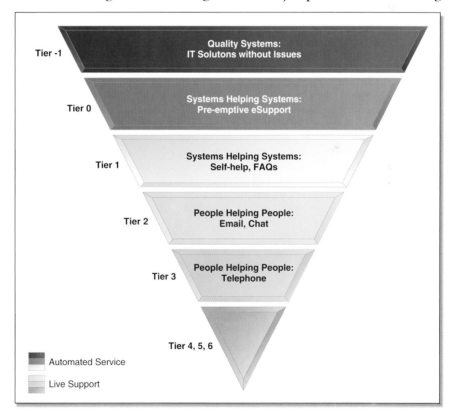

Figure A.3 Eight Tiers of Support

Source: Intel IT, 2007, modified from Forrester Group, 1999

Most importantly, as Figure A.3, shows, they added a tier on top: *Tier -1*. This tier reminds us that higher quality IT solutions will have fewer support needs. Now, there are three tiers that represent automated solutions in the six-level model.

At the bottom of the funnel, Etheredge and Herren added a layer they called *Tier 4, 5, 6.* "We realized that there were other, more highly paid people in the support organization and beyond. From time to time, we need engineering or vendor consultants to help us solve a support problem," Etheredge explained.

Layers and Dollars

"Our eSupport vision has a direct relationship to the cost of handling support incidences," Herren pointed out. "It could easily cost $50 to $100 or more for resources in tiers 4, 5, and 6. This would be a resource we might put to the task of writing or updating a script for our self-help library. With phone support, the cost drops to perhaps $15 to $20 per incident. By leveraging support staff with email and Web technologies, we might be able to reduce the cost of an incident to $1 to $5."

"What's dramatic is that the lifecycle costs of automated systems may be a nickel or a dime per support incidents. Providing our customers with ways to take of themselves results in enormous cost avoidance." Herren concluded.

Epilogue

"One of the goals for the eSupport project was to make a robust customer support system available to others at Intel, and in 2007, this is beginning to take hold." reported Etheredge. "Our Intel product groups are planning to reuse our eSupport infrastructure, primarily to store and evolve their knowledge bases. Our vision that the eSupport technology platform would be useful for other activities at Intel has turned out to be true."

Appendix B

Innovation Assessment Tools

This appendix contains a modified version of Intel's innovation self-assessment tool. We removed some Intel-specific language in the interest of making the tool more useful to a general audience and more easily adaptable to the reader's situation.

A thorough discussion of the self-assessment process, guidelines for scoring within the categories the tool evaluates, and how to develop action plans based on its results can be found in Chapter 6.

This self-assessment instrument will be accessible from the Web site for this book.

Also included at the end of this appendix is a matrix that provides an example of how to incorporate innovation capability maturity in individual performance appraisals.

Intel's Self-Assessment Tool

Section 1. Management Commitment

1.1 Management Involvement

50 points	Examples
■ Evidence of management involvement in innovation	■ An innovation strategy has been defined
	■ Our manager discusses and values innovation
	■ Innovation assessment is conducted annually
	■ Team innovation is recognized and rewarded
■ Areas of potential improvement	■ Management could encourage measured risk taking
	■ Management could set forth an innovation vision
	■ The enterprise could set a corporate innovation goal
	■ Managers and innovators could share decisions

1.2 Communication of Priorities

50 points	Examples
■ Evidence of communicating that innovation is equal to other business priorities	■ Innovation is mentioned in status meetings
	■ Innovation is on the regular staff agenda
	■ Innovation initiatives & projects are widely reported
	■ Innovation is a part of informal conversations
■ Areas of potential improvement	■ Include innovation in management walkarounds
	■ Innovation goals could be in department plans
	■ Innovation articles a part of corporate publications
	■ Include innovation activities in progress reports

1.3 Upward Communications

20 points	Examples
■ Evidence that the importance of innovation is being communicated to the team's management	■ Innovation is mentioned at every status meeting
	■ Innovation is called out in work plans
	■ Managers endorse the team's innovation plans
■ Areas of potential improvement	■ More time could be spent on innovation planning
	■ More budget could be allocated to innovation

1.4 Working Innovation Policy

30 points	Examples
■ Evidence of the existence of an innovation policy or an innovation strategic objective	■ Management is accountable for delivering innovative solutions
	■ Team performance is measured against the innovation policy
	■ Policy is reviewed and updated to a defined schedule

Areas of potential improvement	Policy could be used on a day-by-day basis
	Additional policies could be useful for new disciplines

1.5 Innovation as a Value

30 points	**Examples**
Evidence indicating that innovation is valued by the organization	We have examples of how innovation is valued
	IT leaders communicated the value of innovation
Areas of potential improvement	Stronger ties are needed between innovation and corporate values
	Sharper understanding of benefits is needed

1.6 Resource Allocation

30 points	**Examples**
Evidence that shows that resources are allocated for innovation and how they are allocated.	Three of the team's seven projects involve innovation
	One-third of the team's budget and manpower is dedicated to innovation
	The team has a roadmap showing future innovation investment areas
Areas of potential improvement	More space is needed for innovation prototype testing

1.7 Key Innovation Assets Identified

30 points	**Examples**
Evidence that key innovation assets are identified and described	Our team regularly prepares invention disclosures
	We systematically review patent options for innovations
	Team members have experience with innovation techniques and tools
	Our innovation expertise is documented
	Innovation tools and equipment are available
Areas of potential improvement	A central repository for intellectual property could be helpful
	Innovation prototyping tools could be more robust
	Online access to innovations resources needed
	We could use a dedicated lab for experimenting

Section 2. Business Responsibility

2.1 Organize Staff to Improve Innovation

50 points	Examples
▧ Evidence that IT is organized to support innovation	▧ We have a defined process for investigating novel solutions
▧ Areas of potential improvement	▧ We measure and track the business value of innovations quarterly
	▧ Innovation is an informal process at best
	▧ We don't know whether our innovative systems are returning on our investment
	▧ Investments are sometimes pet projects and are chosen without proper analysis

2.2 Make Innovative Actions and Results Accountable

50 points	Examples
▧ Evidence of accountability for innovation results	▧ Innovative projects are managed with standard methods, milestones, and checkpoints
▧ Areas of potential improvement	▧ Our innovative projects meet their deadlines
	▧ Some projects are cancelled and set aside without review for lessons learned
	▧ We often miss milestones for innovative projects

2.3 Adhere to Enterprise Standards for Innovation

50 points	Examples
▧ Evidence that enterprise standards for innovation are used	▧ We measure ourselves as a level three on our Competency Maturity Framework
	▧ We prototype and benchmark to estimate value and determine investment levels
▧ Areas of potential improvement	▧ Investment decisions are primarily made in the IT organization
	▧ We need to adapt a Competency Maturity Framework for innovation

2.4 Routinely Assess Innovative Initiatives

30 points	Examples
▧ Evidence that assessment activities for innovation initiatives are routinely assessed	▧ We report assessment activities on a monthly basis
▧ Areas of potential improvement	▧ Our action plans include innovation objectives
	▧ Our assessments are informal and irregular
	▧ We need guidance to understand how to increase the quality of our innovation skills

2.5 Involve Employees in Innovation Planning

30 points

Examples

- Evidence that employees are involved in innovation planning
- We include all employees in "map day" where we plan areas of research and investment
- Employee work plans are based on shared organizational objectives

- Areas of potential improvement
- We sometimes assign staff members to projects with little or no input from the employee
- We don't leverage employees' areas of special interest

2.6 Plan for IT Innovation Improvements

30 points

Examples

- Evidence that improvement plans for innovation are used
- We use gap analysis and link findings to action plans

- Areas of potential improvement
- We seek out customer opinion for our goals and plans
- We spend much of our time putting out fires, rather than being strategic and planful
- Our plans lack well-defined business value indicators

2.7 Discuss Innovation in Meetings and Communications

20 points

Examples

- Evidence that innovation activities are being promoted in meetings and communications
- We consult with a marketing and communication person when developing communication
- Innovation is on the agenda for most of our meetings
- We maintain a Web site telling customers what's new and next from our organization

- Areas of potential improvement
- We should bring more innovations into the company from other industries and enterprises
- We could contribute to the corporate newsletter more frequently

Section 3. Innovation Competency

3.1 Innovation Training and Learning Programs

40 points	Examples
▓ Evidence that innovation training and learning is available and built into HR and OD systems	▓ Awareness training for innovation is available
	▓ Our team can access job-specific training
	▓ Innovation is part of IT development plans
	▓ Capturing intellectual property is part of our job
	▓ Innovation is listed as a competency in job training
▓ Areas of potential improvement	▓ Innovation not a part of new hire orientation
	▓ We lack an explicit innovation curriculum
	▓ There are too few workshops on innovation
	▓ Manager training on innovation is lacking

3.2 Innovation Training Improvement Process

20 points	Examples
▓ Evidence of ongoing improvements in innovation training	▓ Innovation training is updated on an annual basis
	▓ New ideas are folded into the curriculum regularly
	▓ Evaluations provide a basis for improvement
	▓ Level 1-4 Kirkpatrick
▓ Areas of potential improvement	▓ The scope of innovation training should be broader
	▓ We have no measures of effectiveness of training
	▓ We should provide feedback on training courses so that instructors can improve them

3.3 Employee Development and Improvement Systems

10 points	Examples
▓ Evidence that demonstrates OD improvement	▓ We link innovation to our focus on quality
	▓ IT skills training is widely advertised and available.
	▓ Surveys are used to evaluate employee development systems and for management performance
	▓ Innovation training is available 24 x 7 to all shifts and locations

Areas of potential improvement	▓ Employee development plans do not include innovation
	▓ Our completion rates are low for innovation training
	▓ We should provide feedback on training courses so that instructors can improve them

Section 4. Enterprise Values

4.1 Communicate Enterprise Values

20 points	Examples
▓ Evidence of communication that corporate values include innovation	▓ We have a clear mission statement that includes innovation
	▓ Our corporate values highlight being innovative
▓ Areas of potential improvement	▓ We don't have an explicit business vision
	▓ While innovation is an enterprise value, it is not integrated with other values

4.2 Seek Customer Input to Products and Services

20 points	Examples
▓ Evidence that customer input is being sought and captured	▓ We have a web site for capturing customer ideas
	▓ Our database of customer ideas is growing rapidly
	▓ We include customers in milestone decisions
	▓ Our customers know where and how to give input
▓ Areas of potential improvement	▓ We don't have a consistent evaluation methodology
	▓ A small percentage of customers provide most of the input
	▓ Assistance center information is not used as an input source

4.3 Utilize Customer Input to Products and Services

20 points	Examples
▓ Evidence that customer input is being used	▓ A third of our innovations were driven by customers
	▓ We maintain a database of customer comments
	▓ Ethnographic surveys
	▓ We conduct observations of customers to see what is needed

Areas of potential improvement	We don't feed complaints into the innovation process
	Many customers are unaware of our interest in input
	We could learn more from the use of help systems

4.4 Measure Customer Input to Products and Services

20 points	**Examples**
Evidence that customer input is being tracked and measured	We track and report the frequency of customer input
	We proactively seek out input on a semi-annual basis
Areas of potential improvement	Response rate for our surveys is only 50%
	We focus our customers on services and not products
	No point of use input is consistently captured

4.5 Include Innovation in Performance Appraisals

20 points	**Examples**
Evidence that individual performance appraisals includes innovative accomplishments	Our appraisal process explicitly identifies innovation
	The appraisal process accepts innovation failures
Areas of potential improvement	IT innovation is subordinated to efficiency mostly
	Criteria for evaluating innovation are vague

4.6 Track Innovation Systematically

20 points	**Examples**
Evidence of systematic monitoring of innovation projects	We monitor innovative projects separately
	Innovative experiments precede deployment
	We publish an innovation portfolio that includes business dial indicators of success
Areas of potential improvement	Our efforts are primarily undirected skunkworks
	We often fail to reuse an innovation in other situations
	We lack a reuse program to reapply assets

4.7 Provide awards for innovation excellence

10 points	**Examples**
Evidence that awards are used to reinforce innovative performance	We have an annual award for the best innovation
	Excellent innovations are highlighted on our web site
	Individuals can nominate others for recognition

Areas of potential improvement	Successes are occasionally rewarded within the group
	Senior managers are often unaware of our good work
	There are gaps in the award process across the organization

4.8 Apply Innovation to the Margin of the Core Business

10 points	Examples
Evidence that innovative projects address more than core business needs	We allocate resources to non-core innovation
	Our management values the importance of innovation throughout the enterprise
	We have time and a place to experiment with innovation
Areas of potential improvement	Only core business investments are made in innovation
	Our teams are territorial and rarely share innovations
	Our IT organization is 100% focused on keeping the business running

4.9 Manage Change and Risk Systematically

10 points	Examples
Evidence that systems are used to expedite change and reduce risk in innovative projects	It is a corporate value that the status quo is not good enough
	We identify risks for innovative projects and manage those risks
	We use pipeline management processes.
Areas of potential improvement	Our team often encounters problems we should have anticipated
	Some senior managers avoid risk whenever possible
	We need a risk management process for innovative IT projects

4.10 Conduct Post-Project Reviews

10 points	Examples
Evidence that reviews are used to draw out lessons learned	Post-mortem review is a part of our methodology
	We pay special attention to expected risks, to see whether our forecasts were correct
	We revisit previous project reviews prior to launching new projects
Areas of potential improvement	We rarely look back at an innovative project
	Post-project reviews are more frequent for successful projects
	Although we file project reviews, we never put them to use

4.11 Track Ideas, Needs, and Challenges Systematically

20 points	Examples
▦ Systems that are in place and are used to track emerging requirements	▦ We use a web-based system to capture ideas, problems, and needs
	▦ We observe our customers doing their work on a regular basis
	▦ We often host campaigns on specific business process topics to seek out needs and challenges
▦ Areas of potential improvement	▦ We have no regular contact with some of our customers
	▦ Most of our customer comments are useless complaints
	▦ We collect ideas, but rarely take action to use them

4.12 Adopt a Failure Management Policy

20 points	Examples
▦ Evidence that methods are used to extract value from totally and partially failed projects	▦ Our management demands useful analysis of projects that encounter problems
	▦ Our motto is "Don't reinvent the wheel, and also don't reinvent the flat tire."
	▦ Our projects are archived for potential re-use
▦ Areas of potential improvement	▦ We rarely dwell on failures
	▦ There is no policy regarding projects that go astray
	▦ We keep legacy systems longer than we should

4.13 Encourage Open Participation in Innovation

20 points	Examples
▦ Specific methods that are used to encourage and entice customers to participate in innovative projects	▦ We have quarterly contests seeking out new ideas from customers
	▦ Line-of-business colleagues are part of our innovation process
	▦ We have a watching brief for innovation at other companies
▦ Areas of potential improvement	▦ New ideas for innovation are the responsibility of an R&D group

---

4.14 Recognize and Reward Innovation Systematically

20 points	Examples
▦ Specific systems that are in place to recognize and reward innovation	▦ Innovation leads to promotions and, sometimes, bonuses
	▦ Our customers rate innovative services and we recognize those who created them

▨ Areas of potential improvement	▨ We have no regular, predictable recognition process
	▨ Management recognizes efficiency, not innovation
	▨ Cash and non-cash reward methods are not in place

4.15 Maintain and Share Goals for Innovation

10 points	**Examples**
▨ Evidence of shared goals for innovation	▨ Providing innovative solutions is part of our mission statement
▨ Areas of potential improvement	▨ Being "fast followers" is a specialty of our team
	▨ We put innovation objectives in our work plans
	▨ We need to develop a shared definition of innovation
	▨ We have not updated our thinking about innovation for 10 years

Section 5. Innovation Support

5.1 Processes for Innovation

70 points	**Examples**
▨ Evidence that processes are used for managing innovation	▨ We have an innovation prototyping laboratory
	▨ Our team knows how to obtain funds for innovative projects
	▨ We have templates for thinking through our diffusion strategy
▨ Areas of potential improvement	▨ Innovation, for us, is ad hoc skunkworks
	▨ It is difficult to find time or funds for innovative projects
	▨ We should plan more workshops on innovation fundamentals

5.2 Use of Innovation Experts

30 points	**Examples**
▨ Evidence that experts are available and utilized to encourage innovation	▨ We consult with innovation experts quarterly
	▨ Mentors of different types are available on an as-needed basis
▨ Areas of potential improvement	▨ Experts are hoarded and are difficult to access
	▨ Innovation expertise as a skill set has not been considered in our organization

---

5.3 Use of IT Systems to Support Innovation

20 points

Examples

▨ Evidence that IT systems in support of innovation are available and are being used

▨ Our on-line tools for sharing ideas and requirements are available with 24 x 7 access

▨ We use content storage technologies to seek re-use opportunities for innovations

▨ Areas of potential improvement

▨ Most of the good ideas are in the heads of IT personnel

▨ Email notes store our ideas, which is a weak approach

5.4 Business Planning and Innovation

20 points

Examples

▨ Evidence that our business plans include innovation

▨ Our strategic plans identify areas where breakthrough information technologies are expected

▨ Innovation is central to our changing business models

▨ Areas of potential improvement

▨ Business planning and innovation are not coordinated activities

▨ We generally minimize spend to improve business profitability

---

Section 6. Impact of Innovation

6.1 Inventory of Innovations

120 points

Examples

▨ Evidences that goals for innovation success are explicitly stated

▨ We use a business value index to measure the potential results of an innovation

▨ Our vision statement maps to objective criteria indicating success

▨ Areas of potential improvement

▨ We often fail to take baseline measures before deploying new systems

▨ For some deployments, we have no measured results

6.2 Business Value of Innovations

120 points

Examples

▨ Evidence that business value of innovations is being measured

▨ We maintain a library of standard business value dials and use them consistently

▨ We run experiments to determine productivity improvements and inform investment decisions

▨ Areas of potential improvement

▨ Finance prepares investment analyses without our input

▨ Some projects are launched without a thoughtful business case

---

Appraising Innovation Performance

Table B.1 Performance Appraisal Matrix for Innovation

Improvement Required	Below Expectations	Successful	Above Expectations	Outstanding
ABSENCE	BEGINNING	DOING	EXCELLENCE	ROLE MODEL
• Does not participate in Innovation activities	• Demonstrates support for innovation activities. • Able to locate corporate and IT innovation on the web.	• Plans or participates on teams that plan innovation activities • Contributes to Innovation COP	• Leads teams that are delivering innovation activities	• Role model for routinely coaching others and leading innovation activities at the division or industry level
• Unable to locate or describe innovation web sites or tools	• Able to locate innovation tools, systems, and resources	• Provides feedback for improving the innovation system	• Shares innovation BKMs and routinely offers improvement suggestions • May deliver innovation content	• Role models innovation practices, tools and solutions by using and sharing them with others • Participates in assessment teams and formally and informally recognizes innovative performance
• Fails to attend innovation training classes	• Attends innovation training classes and begins applying skills	• Attends training classes and consistently applies training skills in the workplace	• Takes responsibility for maintaining and growing innovation skills and coaching of others	• Instructs innovation classes and/or shares innovation expertise
• Uses anti-innovation language, e.g., "this can't be done" and "we've done this before"	• Corrects anti-innovation behavior after being coached	• Recognizes correct innovation behavior and corrects without being coached	• Coaches others in innovative behaviors and acts as a gatekeeper for anti-innovation behavior	• Proactively works with the Innovation and Research teams to raise the bar to achieve a World Class Systemic Innovation System
Does not complete business value forecast for projects	Completes business value forecast behaviors after being coached	Completes business value forecast and corrects it without being coached	Coaches others in completing business value forecasts and consistently delivers BV	• Proactively works on developing business value • Teaches business value classes and/or leads innovation evaluations and assessments • Ensures systems are in place

References

While all publications cited in the book are listed here, please note that this list of references also includes the authors' suggested readings in the current literature on innovation.

Agarwal, R., and Sambamurthy, V. 2002. Principles and Models for Organizing the IT Function, *MIS Quarterly Executive*, Volume 1 (1), March: 1-16.

Alter, A. 2003. Do You Have Any Faith In Your ROI Numbers? *www.cioinsight.com,* March.

Alter, A. 2006. The Bitter Truth About ROI. *www.cioinsight.com*, August 4.

Altshuller, G. 1994. *And Suddenly the Inventor Appeared.* Translated by Lev Shulyak. Worcester, MA: Technical Innovation Center.

Anderson, J., Gimenez, L., Nunley, D., Baldwin, E. 2007. *Developing Systemic Innovation in an IT Organization*, Premier IT Magazine, CXO Media ¨C IDGMA. USA Winter

Andreessen, M. 2002. Sidestepping The New IT Crisis. Tech News/ CNET.com, December.

Baldwin, E. 2004. *Innovation in Industry and Academia.* In B. Fitzgerald and E. Wynn [Eds.] *IT Innovation for Adaptability and Competitiveness*. IFIP TC8/WG8.6 Seventh Working Conference Proceedings, Leixlip, Ireland. Kluwer Academic Publishers.

Barney, J. B. 1991. Firm Resources and Sustained Competitive Advantage. *Journal of Management*, 17;1: 99-120.

Busch, D. 2006. Personal communication.

Chesbrough, H. W. 2003. *Open Innovation: The New Imperative for Creating and Profiting from Technology.* Boston, MA: Harvard Business School Press.

Christensen, C. M. 1997. *The Inventor's Dilemma: When New Technologies Cause Great Firms to Fail.* Boston, MA: Harvard Business School Press.

Covey, S. R. 1989. *The Seven Habits of Highly Effective People.* Simon and Schuster.

Crosby, P. B. 1979. *Quality is free: The Art of Making Quality Certain.* McGraw Hill.

Curley, M. 2004. *Managing Information Technology for Business Value: Practical Strategies for IT and Business Managers.* Hillsboro, OR: Intel Press.

Curley, M. 2006. A Value Based IT Capability Maturity Framework. Intel EMEA Academic Forum, Ireland.

Curley, M. 2006. IT Innovation, A New Era. *Proceedings of the International Conference of Computational Science*, Reading, UK.

Curley, M. 2006. The IT transformation at Intel. *MIS Quarterly Executive*, Volume 5, Issue 4 (1), December. pp. 109-122.

Curley, M. 2007. Introducing the IT Capability Maturity Framework. *Proceedings of the International Conference on Enterprise Information Systems*, Portugal, June.

de Bono, Edward. 1986. *Six Thinking Hats.* London: Penguin Books.

de Geus, A. 1997. *The Living Company: Habits of Survival in a Turbulent Business Environment.* Harvard Business School Press.

Dedrick, J., Gurbaxani, V., and Kraemer, K.L. 2002. Information technology and economic performance: a critical review of the empirical evidence. University of California, Irvine, Center for Research in IT and Organizations (CRITO), November.

Drucker, P. F. 1985. *Innovation and Entrepreneurship.* New York, NY: Harper and Row.

Earl M. J., and Sampler, J. L. 1998. Market Management to Transform the IT Organization. *MIT Sloan Management Review*, Summer.

Eckert, A. 2002. Maximizing ROI Through User Proficiency. Insiders' View, SAS.com, June.

Friedman, T. 2005. *The World is Flat.*New York, NY: Farrar Straus, and Giroux.

Gladwell, Malcolm (2000). *The Tipping Point: How Little Things Can Make a Big Difference.* Little, Brown and Company.

Glass, Gene. 1978. Standards and Criteria. *Journal of Educational Measurement, Vol. 15, No. 4* (Special Issue on Standard Setting), pp. 237-261.

Gurbaxani, V., and Kemerer, C.F. 1990. An Agency Theory View of the Management of Information Systems. *Proceedings of the International Conference on Information Systems*, 279-288.

Humphrey, W. 1989. Managing the Software Process. Software Engineering Institute.

Intel Corporation. 2003. Effects of Wireless Mobile Technology on Employee Productivity: Wireless mobility changes the way employee work. Santa Clara: Intel Corporation. IT@Intel white paper, November. *www.intel.com/it/alpha.htm*.

Intel Corporation. 2004. Business Benefits of Wireless Computing: How wireless improves productivity and return on investment. Santa Clara: Intel Corporation. IT@Intel white paper, September.

Intel Corporation. 2004. Intel Communicates Globally through Instant Messaging. Santa Clara: Intel Corporation. IT@Intel white paper, May. *www.intel.com/it/alpha.htm*.

Intel Corporation. 2004. The Workplace Hits the Road: Intel IT finds its field employees save time, improve productivity using Intel Centrino Mobile Technology. Santa Clara: Intel Corporation. IT@Intel brief, February. *www.intel.com/it/alpha.htm*.

Intel Corporation. 2005. St. Vincent's Hospital Enhances Patient Throughput with RFID and Greater Visibility of Patient Flow. Santa Clara: Intel Corporation. IT@Intel white paper.

Kohli, R., and Deveraj. 2004. Realizing the Business Value of IT Investments: An Organizational Process. *MIS Quarterly Executive*, Volume 3 (1), March.

Marchand, D. A. 2004. Reaping the Business Value of IT: Focus on Usage, Not Just Deployment, To Optimize Payback. IMD publication No. 114, November.

Markus, M.L., and Soh, C. 1993. Banking on Information Technology: Converting IT Spending Into Firm Performance. In R.D Banker, R.J. Kauffman and M.A. Mahmood (Editors), *Strategic Information Technology Management: Perspectives on Organizational growth and Competitive Advantage*. Harrisburg, Pennsylvania: Idea Group Publishing, pp. 405-444.

Markus, M.L., and Soh, C. 1995. How IT Creates Value, a Process Theory Synthesis. *Proceedings of the 16th International Conference of Information Systems*, Amsterdam, The Netherlands.

McNichol, T. 2007. A Startup's Best Friend? Failure from Dogster to Google, Web companies are finding that mistakes can be shortcuts to success. April 4, 2007. *CNNMoney.com*

Mooney, J. G., Gurbaxani, V., and Kraemer, K. 1995. A Process Oriented Framework for Assessing the Business Value of Information Technology. CRITO paper, UC Irvine.

Moore, Geoffrey. 1991/1999. *Crossing the Chasm: Marketing and Selling High-tech Products to Mainstream Customers*.

Mulholland, T., Kurchina, P., and Thomas, C. 2006. *Mashup Corporations, The End of Business as Usual*. Evolve Technology Press.

Paulk, M. C., Curtis, B., Chrissis, M. B., and Weber, C. 1993. Capability Maturity Model for Software, Version 1.1. Software Engineering Institute, CMU/SEI-93-TR-24, DTIC Number ADA263403, February.

Peppard, J., and Ward, J. 2004. Beyond Strategic Information Systems: Towards An IS Capability. *The Journal of Strategic Information Systems*, July, pp. 167-194.

Rogers, E. M. 2003. *Diffusion of Innovations* (Fifth Edition). New York, NY: Free Press.

Ross, J. W., Beath, C. M., and Goodhue, D. L. 1996. Developing Long-term Competitiveness Through Information Technology Assets. *Sloan Management Review*, Vol. 38, Fall.

Ross, J. W., Weill, P., and Robertson, D. C. 2006. *Enterprise Architecture as Strategy: Creating a Foundation for Business Execution*. Harvard Business School Press.

Salman, R., and Younis, N. 2005. Lessons to Management from the Control Loop Phenomenon. *Transactions on Engineering, Computing and Technology.*

Sambamurthy, V., and Zmud, R.W. 1994. IT Management Competency Assessment: A Tool For Creating Business Value Through IT. Working Paper, Financial Executives Research Foundation.

Sward, D. 2006. *Measuring the Business Value of Information Technology: Practical Strategies for IT and Business Managers.* Hillsboro, OR: Intel Press.

Sward, D. 2007 Gaining a Competitive Advantage through User Experience Design. Santa Clara: Intel Corporation. IT@Intel white paper, January. *www.intel.com/it/alpha.htm.*

Tallon, P., et al. 2000. Executives' Perspectives on the Business Value of Information Technology. A Process-Oriented Approach. *Journal of Management Information Systems.*

Thompson, C. 2007. *What a Great Idea 2.0.* Sterling Press.

Thomson, D. 2006. *Blueprint to a Billion.* Hoboken, NJ: , John Wiley.

Tiernan, C., and Peppard, J. 2005. Information Technology: Of Value or a Vulture. *European Management Journal*, 22, 609-623.

Venkatraman, N. 1997. Beyond Outsourcing: Managing IT Resources as a Value Center. *MIT Sloan Management Review*, Spring.

Weill, P. 1992. The Relationship between Investment in Information Technology and Firm Performance: A Study of the Value Manufacturing Sector. *Information Systems Review*, Volume 3, Number 4, 307-333.

Weill, P. 2004. Don't Just Lead, Govern. How Top-performing Firms Govern IT. *MIS Quarterly Executive,* Volume 3 (1), March.

Weill, P., and Ross, J. 2004. *How Top Performers Manage IT Decisions Rights for Superior Results.* Harvard Business School Press.

Weill, P., and Ross, J. 2004. IT Governance in One Page. MIT CISR Working Paper #349.

Weill, P., and Woodham. 2002. Don't Just Lead, Govern: Implementing Effective IT Governance. MIT Sloan CISR Working Paper #326, April.

Index

Continuing Education is Essential

It's a challenge we all face – keeping pace with constant change in information technology. Whether our formal training was recent or long ago, we must all find time to keep ourselves educated and up to date in spite of the daily time pressures of our profession.

Intel produces technical books to help the industry learn about the latest technologies. The focus of these publications spans the basic motivation and origin for a technology through its practical application.

Right books, right time, from the experts

These technical books are planned to synchronize with roadmaps for technology and platforms, in order to give the industry a head-start. They provide new insights, in an engineer-to-engineer voice, from named experts. Sharing proven insights and design methods is intended to make it more practical for you to embrace the latest technology with greater design freedom and reduced risks.

I encourage you to take full advantage of Intel Press books as a way to dive deeper into the latest technologies, as you plan and develop your next generation products. They are an essential tool for every practicing engineer or programmer. I hope you will make them a part of your continuing education tool box.

Sincerely,

Justin Rattner
Senior Fellow and Chief Technology Officer
Intel Corporation

**Turn the page to learn about titles
from Intel Press for system developers**

Managing Information Technology for Business Value

Practical Strategies for IT and Business Managers

By Martin Curley
ISBN 0-9717861-7-8

Managing Information Technology for Business Value is Martin Curley's call for IT and business planners to reformulate the way they manage IT. Traditionally, IT success has been measured in terms of internal IT systems parameters, such as availability, capacity, and processing speed.

It is Curley's contention that if IT is to deliver business value, then IT should be measured in core business terms, such as customer satisfaction, revenue growth, and profitability.

At a time when some corporations are reducing IT spending and once again looking at IT as a cost center, Martin Curley's *Managing Information Technology for Business Value* provides a necessary and timely counterbalance.

The book introduces a capability maturity framework for improving the business value from information technology. The framework includes structured improvement paths and best practices from Intel and the Industry.

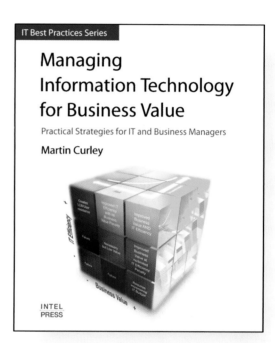

IT Best Practices Series

Managing Information Technology for Business Value

Practical Strategies for IT and Business Managers

Martin Curley

INTEL PRESS

❝ *If you're buying one book on the subject of business value from IT, this is it. Curley shines a light on the path ahead for ambitious users of IT. If you have any impact on how IT gets used in your organization, you owe it to your shareholders to read this book. It will impact your bottom line!* ❞

—*John Fleming, CEO,*
Enzo Consulting

❝ *IT is moving from the back room to the board room—pushing corporations through a strategic inflection point, and presenting CIO's with new and often unforeseen challenges. In this engaging book, Curley offers practical advice and insights into how to respond to these challenges. I consider this book required reading for all IT executives.* ❞

—*Prof. Paul Tallon,*
Carroll School of Management,
Boston College

Measuring the Business Value of Information Technology
Practical Strategies for IT and Business Managers

By David Sward
ISBN 0-9764832-7-0

In today's fast moving competitive business environment, companies increasingly demand that IT investments demonstrate business value through measurable results. Intended for IT professionals and consultants as well as business managers, this book covers one of the most important strategies any company can establish to help manage IT in the coming years. Namely, the creation of an IT Business Value customer focused approaches to determine the business value for any IT investment an organization may make.

Based on financial concepts and drawing on his background as a Human Factors Engineer, Sward makes the case that the process of establishing and running a business value program can ultimately create a new mindset for IT professionals.

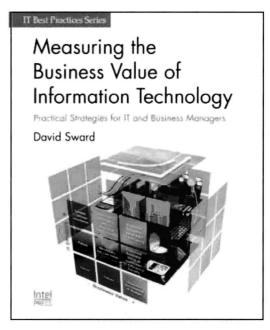

While Sward recognizes this will not happen overnight, he believes it serves to instill a belief that an organization can and will create a competitive advantage and increase shareholder value not by just deploying information technology, but by deploying the *right* information technology by linking IT to corporate objectives and focusing all efforts on the requirements of the end user.

❝David Sward explains the why's, what's, and how's of IT value measurement, presents an intuitively appealing vocabulary, and offers an impressive portfolio of instruments to manage IT investments to produce measured business value. ❞

> —Lars Mathiassen, Professor, Computer Information Systems, Georgia State University

❝Intel's IT Business Value program deserves to be widely emulated. David Sward was one of the program's founders, and he gives the inside details on how it was developed and implemented. This book should influence IT investment and management practices for years to come. ❞

> —Robert Laubacher, Research Associate, MIT Sloan School of Management

Applied Virtualization Technology

Usage Models for IT Professionals and Software Developers

By Sean Campbell and Michael Jeronimo
ISBN: 0-9764832-3-8

Server and desktop virtualization is one of the more significant technologies to impact computing in the last few years, promising the benefits of infrastructure consolidation, lower costs, increased security, ease of management, and greater employee productivity.

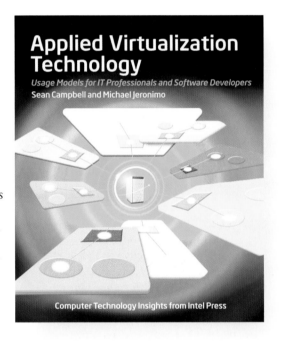

Using virtualization technology, one computer system can operate as multiple "virtual" systems. The convergence of affordable, powerful platforms and robust scalable virtualization solutions is spurring many technologists to examine the broad range of uses for virtualization. In addition, a set of processor and I/O enhancements to Intel server and client platforms, known as Intel® Virtualization Technology (Intel® VT), can further improve the performance and robustness of current software virtualization solutions.

This book takes a user-centered view and describes virtualization usage models for IT professionals, software developers, and software quality assurance staff. The book helps you plan the introduction of virtualization solutions into your environment and thereby reap the benefits of this emerging technology.

Highlights include:

- The challenges of current virtualization solutions
- In-depth examination of three software-based virtualization products
- Usage models that enable greater IT agility and cost savings
- Usage models for enhancing software development and QA environments
- Maximizing utilization and increasing flexibility of computing resources
- Reaping the security benefits of computer virtualization
- Distribution and deployment strategies for virtualization solutions

Service Oriented Architecture Demystified
A pragmatic approach to SOA for the IT executives

By Girish Juneja, Blake Dournaee, Joe Natoli, and Steve Birkel
ISBN 1-934053-02-3

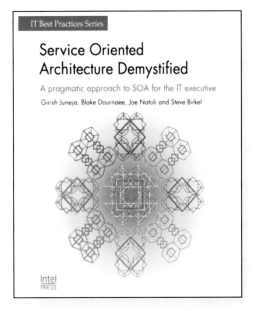

The authors of this definitive book on SOA debunk the myths and demonstrate through examples from different vertical industries how a "crawl, walk, run" approach to deployment of SOA in an IT environment can lead to a successful return on investment.

One popular argument states that SOA is not a technology per se, but that it stands alone and can be implemented using a wide range of technologies. The authors believe that this definition, while attractive and elegant, doesn't necessarily pass pragmatic muster.

Service Oriented Architecture Demystified describes both the technical and organizational impacts of adopting SOA and the pursuant challenges. The authors demonstrate through real life deployments why and how different industry sectors are adopting SOA, the challenges they face, the advantages they have realized, and how they have (or have not) addressed the issues emerging from their adoption of SOA. This book strikes a careful balance between describing SOA as an enabler of business processes and presenting SOA as a blueprint for the design of software systems in general. Throughout the book, the authors attempt to cater to both technical and organizational viewpoints, and show how both are very different in terms of why SOA is useful. The IT software architect sees SOA as a business process enabler and the CTO sees SOA as a technology trend with powerful paradigms for software development and software integration.

SOA can be characterized in terms of different vertical markets. For each such market, achieving SOA means something different and involves different transformational shifts. The vertical markets covered include healthcare, government, manufacturing, finance, and telecommunications. SOA considerations are quite different across these vertical markets, and in some cases, the required organizational shifts and technology shifts are highly divergent and context dependent.

Whether you are a CTO, CIO, IT manager, or IT architect, this book provides you with the means to analyze the readiness of your internal IT organization and with technologies to adopt a service oriented approach to IT.

Enhance security and protection against software-based attacks

The Intel Safer Computing Initiative

Building Blocks for Trusted Computing

By David Grawrock

ISBN 0-9764832-6-2

With the ever-increasing connectivity of home and business computers, it is essential that developers understand how the Intel Safer Computing Initiative can provide critical security building blocks to better protect the PC computing environment. Security capabilities need to be carefully evaluated before delivery into the marketplace. Intel is committed to delivering security capabilities in a responsible manner for end users and the ecosystem.

A highly versatile set of hardware-based security enhancements, code-named LaGrande Technology (LT), will be supported on Intel processors and chipsets to help enhance PC platforms. This book covers the fundamentals of LT and key Trusted Computing concepts such as security architecture, cryptography, trusted computer base, and trusted channels.

Highlights include:

- History of trusted computing and definitions of key concepts
- Comprehensive overview of protections that are provided by LaGrande Technology
- Case study showing how access to memory is the focal point of an attack
- Protection methods for execution, memory, storage, input, and graphics
- How the Trusted Platform Module (TPM) supports attestation

In this concise book, the lead security architect for Intel's next-generation security initiative provides critical information you need to evaluate Trusted Computing for use on today's PC systems and to prepare your designs to respond to future threats.

Multi-Core Programming
Increasing Performance through Software Multi-threading

By Shameem Akhter and Jason Roberts

ISBN 0-9764832-4-6

Software developers can no longer rely on increasing clock speeds alone to speed up single-threaded applications; instead, to gain a competitive advantage, developers must learn how to properly design their applications to run in a threaded environment. This book helps software developers write high-performance multi-threaded code for Intel's multi-core architecture while avoiding the common parallel programming issues associated with multi-threaded programs. This book is a practical, hands-on volume with immediately usable code examples that enable readers to quickly master the necessary programming techniques.

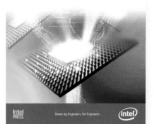

Multi-Core Programming
Increasing Performance through Software Multi-threading
Shameem Akhter and Jason Roberts

Intel PRESS   Books by Engineers, for Engineers   (intel)

Discover programming techniques for Intel multi-core architecture and Hyper-Threading Technology

The Software Optimization Cookbook, Second Edition
High-Performance Recipes for IA-32 Platforms

By Richard Gerber, Aart J.C. Bik, Kevin B. Smith, and Xinmin Tian

ISBN 0-9764832-1-1

Four Intel experts explain the techniques and tools that you can use to improve the performance of applications for IA-32 processors. Simple explanations and code examples help you to develop software that benefits from Intel® Extended Memory 64 Technology (Intel® EM64T), multi-core processing, Hyper-Threading Technology, OpenMP*, and multimedia extensions. This book guides you through the growing collection of software tools, compiler switches, and coding optimizations, showing you efficient ways to get the best performance from software applications.

The Software Optimization Cookbook
High-Performance Recipes for IA-32 Platforms
Richard Gerber, Aart J.C. Bik, Kevin B. Smith, and Xinmin Tian
Second Edition

Intel PRESS   Books by Engineers, for Engineers   (intel)

" *A must-read text for anyone who intends to write perform- ance-critical applica- tions for the Intel processor family.* "

—Robert van Engelen,
Professor,
Florida State University

Special Deals, Special Prices!

To ensure you have all the latest books
and enjoy aggressively priced discounts,
please go to this Web site:

www.intel.com/intelpress/bookbundles.htm

Bundles of our books are available,
selected especially to address the needs
of the developer. The bundles place
important complementary topics at
your fingertips, and the price for a
bundle is substantially less than
buying all the books individually.